Contents

HISTORY

COUNTRIES

Human beings

There are more than 6.4 billion people on Earth. No one else is exactly like you, but everyone has a body that is made up of the same basic parts.

The parts of the human body work together to keep you alive.

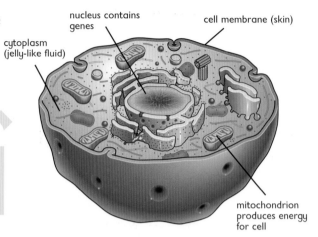

▽ Inside a cell in your body. Most cells are about 0.02 mm across.

nucleus contains genes

cell membrane (skin)

cytoplasm (jelly-like fluid)

mitochondrion produces energy for cell

Genes

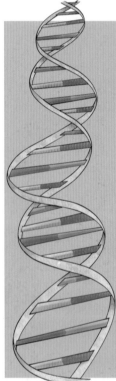

Genes are the instructions that make you who you are. Every cell in your body contains a copy of your genes. Each gene is one section of a long strand of DNA. Under a microscope, DNA looks like a long ladder, twisted into a spiral.

◁◁ Strand of DNA.

Building blocks of life

Like all living things, the human body is made up of tiny building blocks, called cells. Your body contains billions of cells, each so small it can only be seen through a microscope.

△ Your skin gets its colour from a chemical called melanin. People with dark skin have more melanin than people with light skin.

Tissues and organs

Groups of similar cells that work together are called tissues. Nerve tissues and muscle tissues are two examples.

The organs in your body, such as your heart and brain, are made up of different kinds of tissue that work together.

Your working body

Some groups of organs and tissues work together in systems to do particular jobs.

▽ **The systems of the body.**

1. Your brain, spinal cord and nerves make up the nervous system, that controls your body and carries information. Find out more on page 15.

2. Your heart, blood vessels and blood carry oxygen to every part of the body, and carry away waste. Find out more on page 10.

3. Your kidneys and bladder take waste from the blood out of the body in your urine.

4. Your digestive system takes the goodness from food. Find out more on page 11.

5. Your windpipe and lungs take in oxygen from the air when you breathe. Find out more on page 9.

6. Your bones give your body its shape. Find out more on page 8.

7. Your muscles work with your bones so that you can move. Find out more on page 8.

Skin

Your body is protected by a waterproof covering of skin. Skin stops your body from losing water. You also touch things through your skin. The fine hairs that grow from your skin help to keep your body warm. The sweat pores on your skin help to cool you down when you are too hot.

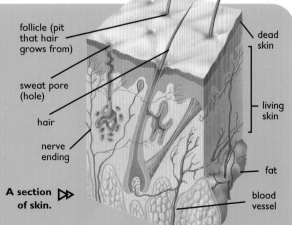

A section ▷▷ **of skin.**

follicle (pit that hair grows from)

sweat pore (hole)

hair

nerve ending

dead skin

living skin

fat

blood vessel

Bones and muscles

Inside your body is a skeleton of over 200 bones. There are bones in your arms, your legs and even your ears. Each bone has muscles attached to it, so you can move in amazing ways.

If you didn't have muscles, you wouldn't be able to run, jump, hop or dance, which would be no fun at all!

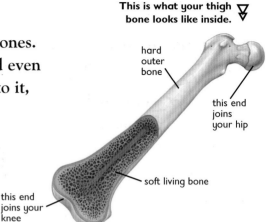

This is what your thigh bone looks like inside. ▽

hard outer bone

this end joins your hip

soft living bone

this end joins your knee

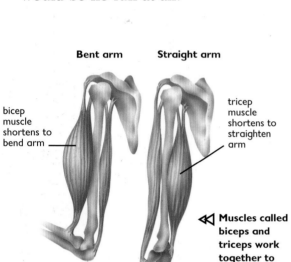

Bent arm

Straight arm

bicep muscle shortens to bend arm

tricep muscle shortens to straighten arm

◄◄ **Muscles called biceps and triceps work together to bend and straighten your arm.**

Muscles and moving

Muscles attached to your bones make you move. When they shorten, they pull the bone one way. You have other types of muscle, too – your heart is one big muscle!

Joints

When you sit down, walk or jump, you bend your knees. When you pick something up, you bend your arm or wrist. These bends, called joints, are where your bones meet.

Inside bones

Bones are partly made of a hard, stony substance called calcium which makes them amazingly strong. Your bones also have living cells inside them so that they can mend themselves if they get broken.

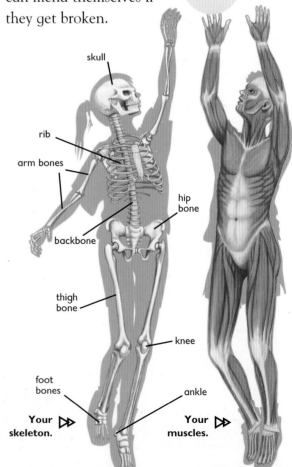

skull

rib

arm bones

hip bone

backbone

thigh bone

knee

foot bones

ankle

Your ▷▷ skeleton.

Your ▷▷ muscles.

Breathing

As you read this book, you are breathing. It's what keeps you alive. You take 20,000 breaths a day – that's a lot of breathing!

All human beings need a gas called oxygen to live. There is oxygen in the air all around you.

In and out

When you breathe in, your lungs fill with air. The oxygen in that air goes into your blood and travels around your body, giving you energy.

When you breathe out, you push the air out again. All the oxygen has gone. In its place is a gas your body doesn't need, called carbon dioxide.

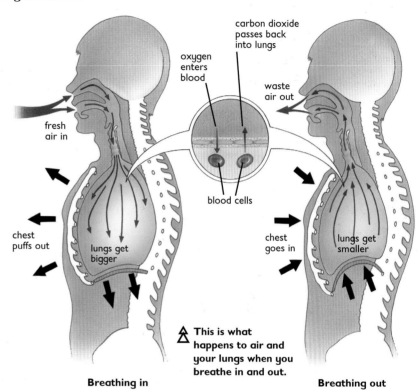

oxygen enters blood

carbon dioxide passes back into lungs

waste air out

fresh air in

blood cells

chest puffs out

lungs get bigger

chest goes in

lungs get smaller

⚠ This is what happens to air and your lungs when you breathe in and out.

Breathing in

Breathing out

Lungs

Your two lungs are protected by bones called ribs. Below your lungs is a muscle called a diaphragm. When you take a breath, your diaphragm moves down and your ribs move outwards to give your lungs the space to get bigger. Fold your arms across your chest and breathe in to feel this happen.

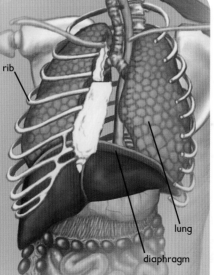

rib

lung

diaphragm

DID YOU KNOW?

When you're asleep, you breathe more slowly than when you're awake. Your body doesn't need so much oxygen when it's still. When you run, your body needs a lot more oxygen – so your breathing speeds up.

Heart and blood

Your heart beats non-stop, 24 hours a day and seven days a week. If you live to be 70 years old, that comes to more than 2.5 billion heartbeats!

The heart pumps blood around the body through tubes called blood vessels.

Vessels, arteries and veins

Blood carrying oxygen away from the heart travels along thick-walled vessels called arteries. Once the oxygen has been removed, the blood returns to the heart through thinner-walled vessels called veins.

How the heart works

The right side of the heart receives blood from the body and pumps it into the lungs, where it can pick up oxygen. The blood returns to the left side of the heart, which pumps it to organs and muscles all over the body.

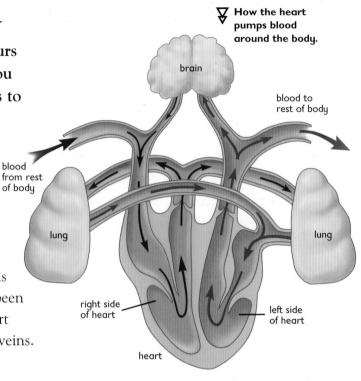

▽ How the heart pumps blood around the body.

brain

blood to rest of body

blood from rest of body

lung

lung

right side of heart

left side of heart

heart

▽ Blood takes waste away from the body's cells. Your kidney removes the waste, through tiny tubes called nephrons.

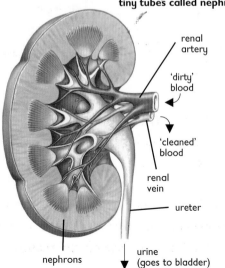

renal artery

'dirty' blood

'cleaned' blood

renal vein

ureter

nephrons

urine (goes to bladder)

Blood

Human blood contains different kinds of cell. Red blood cells carry oxygen. White blood cells (coloured blue here) fight disease. Platelets (coloured cream here) help cuts to scab over.

Human blood cells ▽ under a microscope.

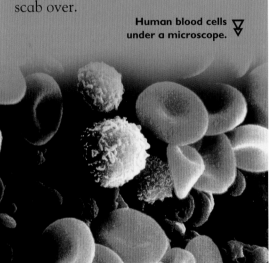

Food and digestion

You need food to live and grow. Your body breaks it down and takes out the goodness that it can use. This is called digestion.

You digest food in a long tube – your gut – which stretches from your mouth to your anus.

△ Bread is a common food in many parts of the world.

From mouth to stomach

When you eat, you chew the food into pieces that are small enough to swallow. These travel down a tube called the gullet into your stomach, where special juices (acids and enzymes) break down the food.

Cross-section ▽
of a tooth. ▽

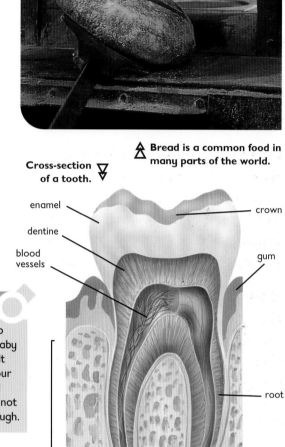

enamel

dentine

blood
vessels

crown

gum

root

jawbone

nerve

Your digestive ▽
system. ▽

DID YOU KNOW?

Humans grow two sets of teeth: 20 baby teeth, and 32 adult teeth. The back four adult teeth (called wisdom teeth) do not always come through.

mouth

gullet

liver stores
extra food

stomach

pancreas
makes
digestive
juices

small
intestine

large
intestine

rectum

From stomach to rectum

From the stomach, broken-up food moves through the small intestine. Useful nutrients pass through its walls and into the blood, to be carried to the rest of the body. What is left of the food continues into the large intestine and leaves the body through the rectum.

Reproduction and growth

Like all animals, humans can reproduce – make new human beings. In humans, there are two different sexes, males and females. A male and female cell must come together in order to create a new human.

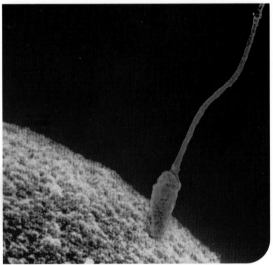

New life begins when a sperm cell meets an egg inside the mother's body.

Sperm and egg

A male cell is called a sperm and a female cell is called an egg.

Each cell carries genes – instructions that help to build a living thing. A baby starts out as a cell from each parent, so it contains genes from each parent.

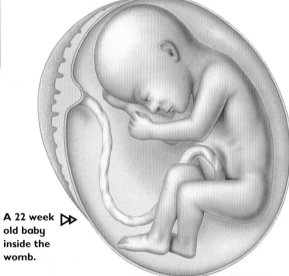

A 22 week old baby inside the womb.

Life begins

When a sperm joins with an egg, a baby can begin to grow. It develops inside the mother's womb for around nine months. When it is ready to be born, it is pushed out of the mother's body.

Twins

Two babies that develop together in the womb are called twins. Sometimes they grow from two separate eggs. Sometimes, they come from a single egg that splits in two. When this happens, the babies share the same genes. They are called identical twins.

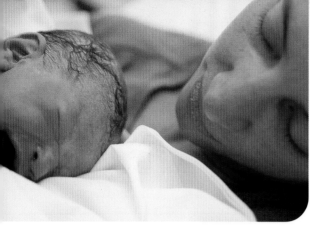

Babies and children

Babies depend on their parents for everything. At about a year old, they become toddlers, able to walk by themselves. Soon they develop into little boys and girls.

The time when you are a baby and child is when you do most of your growing and learning.

▲ Newborn babies depend on their mother for food and warmth.

Aged one, a baby can stand, or even walk.

At three years, a child can join in conversations.

▽ Children learn different skills at different ages.

At four months, a baby can smile and hold toys.

Aged six, a child learns to read and write.

At 12 years, a child can learn and discover on her own.

From child to adult

Puberty is when your body changes from a child's to an adult's. It usually begins in your early teens and goes on until you are between 16 and 20 years old. The changes make it possible for you to have babies of your own one day.

Growing older

When you are an adult, your body stops growing taller, but it still changes. Over time, people's muscles and bones become weaker. Women can no longer have babies. When people get very old, their bodies wear out and they die.

In rich countries, most people live to about 75 years old. In the poorest parts of the world, people may only live to about 45 years old.

How girls develop into adults. ▽

baby

toddler

child

adolescent (at puberty)

young adult

How boys develop into adults. ▽

baby

toddler

child

adolescent (at puberty)

young adult

Senses

Your senses tell you what is going on in the world around you.

The eyes, ears, skin, nose and tongue are your sense organs. They gather information and send it along nerves to the brain. The brain turns it into sights, sounds, touches, smells and tastes.

How eyes see

Light bounces off everything around you. It enters the eye through the pupil (the black dot in the middle).

At the back of the eye, light is turned into nerve signals that travel to the brain. The brain changes the signals into pictures.

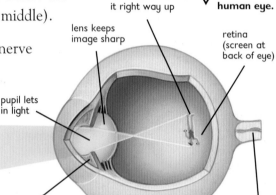

image is upside down: brain turns it right way up

▽ **Inside the human eye.**

lens keeps image sharp

retina (screen at back of eye)

pupil lets in light

iris (coloured part of eye)

nerve carries signal to brain

How ears hear

The ear's shell shape collects sounds and channels them into the eardrum. Sounds make the parts of the ear vibrate (wobble very fast). This moves tiny hairs in the inner ear, that are attached to nerves. They send information about the sounds to the brain.

◁◁ Braille is a special kind of writing for blind people. The letters are raised dots that can be read by touch.

Many deaf people use their hands to talk. This is called signing. ▷▷

Brain and nerves

The brain is the body's control centre. Nerves carry messages between the brain and the rest of the body. Nerves reach out from your spinal cord to every part of the body.

Together, the brain, spinal cord and nerves make up the nervous system.

Nerves

Nerves carry information to the brain, such as messages about your surroundings from your eyes and other sense organs. The brain uses this information to decide how your body will behave. The brain sends out instructions to the body along the nerves.

Neurons

Inside the brain, nerve cells called neurons store information – and also share it, by linking up with each other.

Different parts of the brain carry out different jobs. The biggest part of the brain, the cerebrum, looks after thought and memory.

Reflexes

Your body does some things without you thinking about them. If you touch something hot, you pull away your hand straight away. This is called a reflex action.

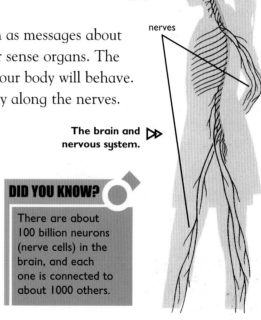

central nervous system
brain
spinal cord
nerves

The brain and ▷▷ nervous system.

DID YOU KNOW?

There are about 100 billion neurons (nerve cells) in the brain, and each one is connected to about 1000 others.

The different parts ▽ of the brain. ▽

What the areas of ▽ the brain look after. ▽

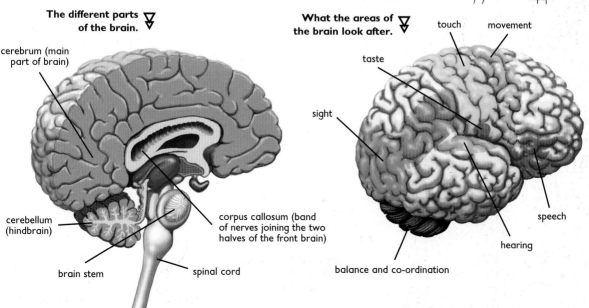

cerebrum (main part of brain)

cerebellum (hindbrain)

brain stem

spinal cord

corpus callosum (band of nerves joining the two halves of the front brain)

touch   movement

taste

sight

speech

hearing

balance and co-ordination

Health and fitness

To stay healthy and fit you need to look after your body. That means eating well and taking regular exercise.

The place where you live also affects your health. People live longer, healthier lives in parts of the world where there is a clean water supply and good medical care.

A healthy diet

Eating well is also called having a balanced diet. Carbohydrates, such as pasta, bread and rice, give the body energy. Fruit and vegetables help the body to fight disease. Your body needs proteins, found in meat, fish and cheese, so it can build new cells.

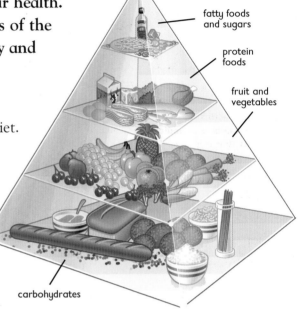

▽ The foods that make up a healthy diet. You should eat more of the foods at the bottom of the pyramid and less of the foods at the top.

fatty foods and sugars

protein foods

fruit and vegetables

carbohydrates

Health care

Doctors and nurses treat you when you are sick. They can also help you to stay healthy. They can protect you against some diseases with injections (jabs). They may watch your weight so they can pick up early signs of sickness.

A nurse weighs a baby. ▽

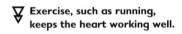
▽ Exercise, such as running, keeps the heart working well.

Exercise

Keeping fit helps to keep your body healthy. There are lots of different ways to exercise – walking, running, cycling, swimming and playing football.

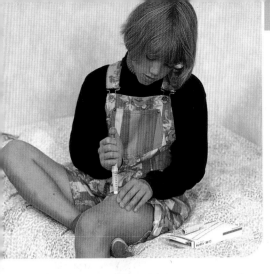

Diseases

The common cold is a disease that makes you feel rotten, but does no lasting harm. Other diseases, such as diabetes, are serious but they can be controlled with drugs. But some diseases, such as cancer or Aids, can kill.

The causes of many diseases – and how to treat them – are still not known.

△ People with diabetes do not produce insulin, a chemical that bodies need. Diabetics inject themselves with insulin every day.

Where disease comes from

People may be born with a disease or they may get one from an infection or some other cause. Infectious diseases are spread by germs such as bacteria, viruses and fungi.

Some germs spread through the air when people cough or sneeze. Others live in dirty food or water. Some can be passed on by touch.

Louis Pasteur (1822–1895) was a French △ scientist who discovered that tiny living things called bacteria cause diseases.

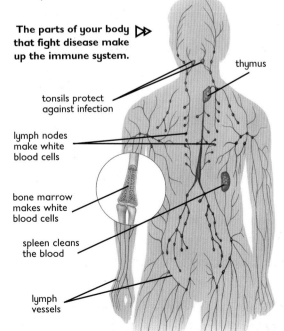

The parts of your body ▷▷ that fight disease make up the immune system.

thymus

tonsils protect against infection

lymph nodes make white blood cells

bone marrow makes white blood cells

spleen cleans the blood

lymph vessels

FAST FACTS ▷▷

- Food poisoning, whooping cough and TB are all diseases caused by bacteria.
- Aids, measles, chicken pox, flu and colds are all diseases caused by viruses.
- Athlete's foot and ringworm are diseases caused by fungi.

Mental illness

Diseases of the mind are called mental illness. They may make people behave in an unusual way, or see or hear things that are not there. Doctors called psychiatrists treat mental illness.

Life on Earth

From tiny bacteria to huge blue whales, all living things grow, reproduce and adapt to their surroundings.

The first life forms were like bacteria and appeared on Earth over 3500 million years ago. They probably lived in pockets of muddy water, warmed by volcanoes.

These are the remains of huge colonies of bacteria, which were some of Earth's earliest life forms.

Early life forms

After millions of years, some living things began to use the Sun's energy to make food. They took in carbon dioxide gas from the air and gave off oxygen. Oxygen – the gas that all animals need to live – became part of the air.

DID YOU KNOW?

Not all animal fossils are bits of bone or shell. There are fossilized droppings and footprints, too.

These fossils are ammonites – shelled sea creatures that lived between 400 and 64 million years ago.

Animals

The first animals were simple, with just one cell. More complicated animals, such as sponges and jellyfish, appeared over 600 million years ago.

Life in the sea

About 570 million years ago, some animals grew hard shells. Shells make good fossils, so we know a lot about these animals. Some have died out now.

The first fish appeared 500 million years ago. They developed into the sharks and other fish we know today.

Some of the life on Earth during the last 600 million years.

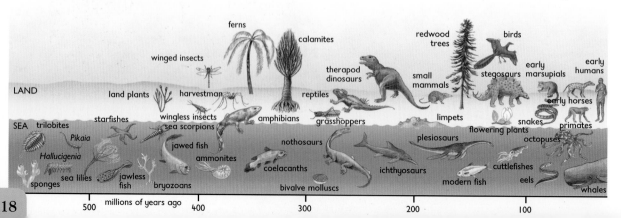

ferns
calamites
redwood trees
birds
winged insects
therapod dinosaurs
small mammals
stegosaurs
early marsupials
early humans
LAND
land plants
harvestman
reptiles
early horses
wingless insects
amphibians
grasshoppers
limpets
snakes
primates
SEA trilobites
starfishes
sea scorpions
flowering plants
octopuses
Pikaia
jawed fish
nothosaurs
plesiosaurs
Hallucigenia
ammonites
cuttlefishes
sponges
sea lilies
jawless fish
bryozoans
coelacanths
ichthyosaurs
modern fish
eels
bivalve molluscs
whales

500   millions of years ago   400   300   200   100

A kingdom is a huge ▷▷ group of life forms that share things in common. Scientists split life forms into five kingdoms.

THE FIVE KINGDOMS

Monera (bacteria and blue-green algae): 4000 kinds

bacteria

blue-green algae

Protoctista (protozoa and algae): 80,000 kinds

amoeba

heliozoan

Fungi: 72,000 kinds

fly agaric mushroom

Plants: 270,000 kinds

Animals: 1,320,000 kinds

moss

Scots pine

lugworm

rat

spore-producing

tulip

flowering

cone-bearing

spider

swallow

sea anemone

frog

without backbones

with backbones

shark

Life on land

About 400 million years ago, small plants, fungi and insects began to live alongside water. In time, plants covered the land. They were food for many different animals.

Reptiles

The first reptiles appeared 280 million years ago. Some lived in water and some flew through the air. Dinosaurs were reptiles that lived on land – and some of them were enormous! Ultrasaurus weighed 120 tonnes.

Mammals and birds

Mammals appeared at the same time as early dinosaurs. Birds came later. They were related to small, meat-eating dinosaurs.

Around 65 million years ago, dinosaurs died out. Mammals became the biggest kingdom (group) of living things.

◁◁ Ninety-nine per cent of all the kinds of animal that have ever lived have now died out. Woolly mammoths died out 10,000 years ago.

How fossils form

Fossils are the remains of living things that died millions of years ago. This is how they form:

1. When an animal dies, it sinks to the seabed. Most of its remains are eaten, but its hard parts are left.
2. Sand and mud bury the remains. Minerals in the sea water replace the hard parts.
3. Slowly, water is squeezed out of the sand and mud and it becomes hard rock.
4. Millions of years later, the rock may be part of dry land. Rain, wind or the sea wear it away and uncover the fossil.

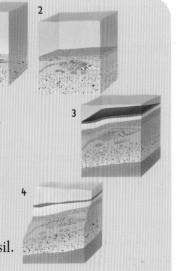

Plants

Plants include the biggest and oldest living things on Earth. Unlike animals, plants stay in one place, usually rooted in the ground. Also unlike animals, plants are able to make their own food. They do this inside their leaves.

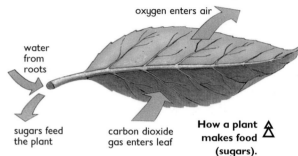

energy from sunlight

Making food

A plant takes in carbon dioxide gas from the air through its leaves. It also takes in water from the ground through its roots. Leaves use the energy in sunlight to turn this carbon dioxide and water into sugars – food for the plant. As a waste product, plants make oxygen, which goes back into the air.

oxygen enters air

water from roots

sugars feed the plant

carbon dioxide gas enters leaf

How a plant makes food (sugars).

⚠ **The Venus fly-trap is a plant that eats insects! It catches them between its snap-shut leaves.**

Other foods

A few plants do not bother to make their own food. Mistletoe grows on trees and uses special suckers to steal food and water.

Some plants need extra food because they live on poor soil. Meat-eating plants trap insects or other small creatures.

▽ **Some types of tree.**

The biggest plants

Trees are the biggest plants – some are over 100 metres tall. Some trees keep their leaves all year round. They are called evergreens. Some lose their leaves for part of the year. They are called deciduous trees.

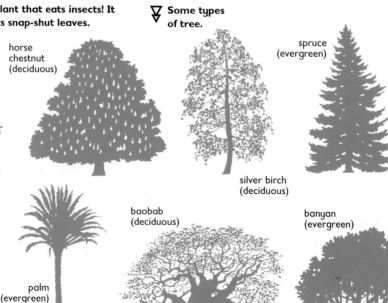

horse chestnut (deciduous)

spruce (evergreen)

silver birch (deciduous)

palm (evergreen)

baobab (deciduous)

banyan (evergreen)

Spreading by seeds

Plants have different ways of reproducing. Flowering plants make male and female sex cells in their flowers. Animals or the wind carry the male sex cells (called pollen) to the female sex cells of another flower. When the sex cells join, they make a seed.

Conifers also have tiny flowers that spread pollen. Conifers produce seeds on woody cones. When the cone opens, the wind spreads the seeds.

Plant lookalikes

Many seaweeds look like plants and even make their own food using the energy from sunlight – but they are not plants. They belong to the group of living things called algae. Mushrooms and toadstools also look like plants, but they are types of fungus.

△ **Green seaweed**

FAST FACTS ▶▶

Tallest plant:
Coast redwood (111 m)
Fastest-growing plant:
Giant bamboo (90 cm per day)
Biggest seed:
Double coconut (20 kg)

Spreading by spores

Ferns, mosses and liverworts do not make seeds. They spread by tiny, dust-like particles called spores. Look on the back of a fern's fronds. The brown dots are where the fern makes its spores.

△ **Moss is a very simple kind of plant. It does not have proper roots.**

▽ **Plants include mosses, liverworts, ferns, conifers and flowering plants.**

SPORE-PRODUCING PLANTS

Mosses and liverworts produce spores in box-like capsules. There are about 16,000 kinds.

Ferns reproduce by spores, formed on the underside of their fronds (leaves). There are about 10,000 kinds.

liverwort

fern

moss

CONE-BEARERS

monkey-puzzle tree

cone

Conifers and their relatives produce cones that contain their seeds. There are about 500 kinds.

FLOWERING PLANTS

monocots

Monocots are flowering plants that make seeds with one pre-packed leaf. There are 50,000 kinds.

grass

tulip

dicots

oak tree

sunflower

Dicots are flowering plants that make seeds with two pre-packed leaves. There are 190,000 kinds.

THE PLANT KINGDOM

Flowers and fruit

Flowers are lovely to look at and fruit is delicious to eat. But flowers and fruit are not just there for us to enjoy. They do a very important job for plants – they allow them to reproduce.

Flowering plants make up the biggest group of plants. There are about 240,000 kinds.

Parts of a flower

All flowers have the same basic parts. Their petals are often colourful and scented. Stamens in the middle of the flower carry its male sex cells, called pollen. Carpels contain the female sex cells, called ovules.

Key

1 carpel
2 petal
3 sepal
4 stamen
5 anther (contains pollen)
6 ovary (contains ovule)
7 stigma (receives pollen)
8 bud
9 fruit
10 seed
11 leaf makes food for plant
12 stem supports plant
13 root sucks up water

△ Parts of a flowering plant.

This grass plant is flowering. It does not need showy flowers, because the wind spreads its pollen. ▽

◁ Pretty or scented flowers, such as roses, use animals to spread their pollen.

Pollination

For a seed to form, pollen has to join with an ovule from another flower. This is called pollination. Some plants use the wind to carry their pollen to other flowers. Some plants use animals, such as bees or butterflies.

Flowers attract animals with a sweet, sugary drink called nectar. As they drink, pollen sticks to the animals' bodies. They carry it to the next flower they visit.

Making seeds

Once two sex cells have joined, the flower can grow a seed. The ovary swells up to form a fruit. The fruit protects the seeds and also helps them to spread.

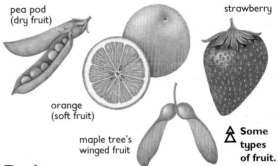

pea pod
(dry fruit)

strawberry

orange
(soft fruit)

maple tree's
winged fruit

△ Some
types
of fruit.

Fruits

Animals eat soft, juicy fruits. The seeds come out in their droppings. Dry fruits are seed heads with dry or papery cases. Some, called burs, have tiny hooks that stick to fur or feathers.

The wind spreads many plants' seeds. Some trees produce seeds with papery wings. The fruits of dandelions and thistles have parachutes.

△ A meadow of wild flowers in South Africa.

▽ The fruiting bodies of three types of fungus.

DID YOU KNOW?

A rainforest plant called rafflesia has the world's biggest flowers. Each one is around 60 cm across — about the size of a dinner plate!

Fungus fruits

Mushrooms and toadstools are fungi, not plants. Instead of making seeds, they reproduce by making tiny spores. The part of the fungus that makes spores is called the fruiting body. It is only a small part of the whole fungus — most of it is hidden underground in a huge tangle of tiny threads.

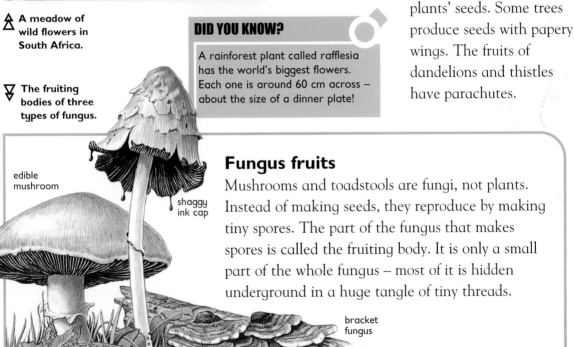

edible
mushroom

shaggy
ink cap

bracket
fungus

Animals

There are millions of different kinds of animals. Some are huge and some can only be seen with a microscope.

All animals have certain things in common. Unlike plants, they cannot make their own food. They have to eat plants or other animals. Animals also need oxygen to survive. They can reproduce and they can move about.

Scientists split the animal kingdom into two groups – animals with backbones and animals without backbones.

mammals

birds

mouse

koala

chimpanzee

reptiles

thrush

lizard

tern

amphibians

tortoise

newt

frog

9000 kinds

4000 kinds

fish

6000 kinds

4000 kinds

stingray

European brown trout

21,000 kinds

with backbones

THE ANIMAL KINGDOM

starfish and their relatives

starfish

sea urchin

5000 kinds

without backbones

arthropods

crab

beetle

spider

1,180,000 kinds

45,000 kinds

molluscs

snail

squid

7000 kinds

earthworm

segmented worms

nematode

12,000 kinds

10,000 kinds

7000 kinds

10,000 kinds

roundworms

flatworm

jellyfish

flatworms and flukes

fluke

sea anemone

sponge

jellyfish and their relatives

sponges

△ A green turtle travels 2000 km to reach the island where it breeds. This sort of long, regular journey is called migration.

Reproduction

All animals can produce young. Usually, males and females must mate. Some animals, such as sea anemones, split off pieces of their own bodies to produce young.

Keeping warm

Birds and mammals can control their body temperature. This is called being warm-blooded. Most animals are cold-blooded. They have to warm up in the sun before they can move around.

◁◁ Many animals use camouflage to hide. This leaf insect is disguised to look like a leaf.

FAST FACTS

◎ The largest animal is the blue whale. It can weigh over 100 tonnes.
◎ The largest land animal is the African elephant. It weighs up to 8 tonnes.
◎ The tallest animal is the giraffe. It stands up to 5.3 m tall.

Squids, snails and shellfish

Squids, snails and shellfish all belong to a family of animals called molluscs. They have a soft, boneless body and, sometimes, a shell.

Most molluscs live in the sea, but some live in rivers or lakes. A few, such as garden snails, live on land.

Armed hunters

Squids and octopuses have eight arms covered in suckers. Octopuses use theirs to catch prey. Squids' arms are shorter. They catch their prey with two long tentacles.

Snails and slugs

There are over 35,000 kinds of slugs and snails. They walk or swim using a large, muscly foot. Land snails and slugs move along a trail of slime.

Shellfish

Mussels, oysters and scallops are all molluscs that have a two-part shell. They feed by taking tiny scraps of plants and animals from the water.

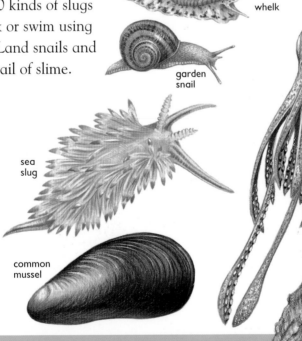

octopus

whelk

garden snail

sea slug

squid

common mussel

◁◁ Some different kinds of mollusc.

An oyster closes its shell when it is in danger. ▽

Oysters and pearls

If a grain of sand gets inside its shell, an oyster covers it with a smooth, pearly substance, to stop it rubbing. In time, the layers build up and the grain becomes a pearl.

Crabs and their relatives

Crabs belong to a family of animals called crustaceans ("crusty ones"). Other crustaceans include lobsters, prawns, barnacles and woodlice. All of these animals have hard armour or a shell.

Most crustaceans live in the sea or freshwater. A few, such as woodlice, live on land.

◁◁ Barnacles attach themselves to rocks and boats. Their feet comb the water for food.

◁◁ Daphnia are water fleas.

Great and small

There are around 150,000 different kinds of crustacean. Lobsters, which can weigh up to 20 kilograms, are the biggest. Copepods, which are less than a millimetre long, are the smallest.

△ There are over 3000 kinds of woodlouse.

▽ Crabs have five pairs of legs and can walk in any direction.

Lobsters use their big claws to crush and tear up prey. △△

Life cycles

Crabs and other sea-living crustaceans produce thousands of tiny young, called larvae. They are swept along by ocean currents and many are eaten.

Adult crustaceans settle in one area. As they grow, they shed (lose) and regrow their shell many times.

Plankton

Tiny, shrimp-like crustaceans called krill are very important in the food chain. They feed on the smallest plants and animals in the oceans. In turn, they are food for larger animals such as birds, seals, whales and sharks.

Spiders and scorpions

Spiders and scorpions may be creepy-crawlies, but they are not insects. They have eight legs, not six, and have two main body parts, not three.

Spiders and scorpions are hunters. They live by catching small insects and other creatures to eat.

Spiders

So far, we know of 30,000 kinds of spider. Spiders produce silk for webs, traps and protecting their eggs. When spider eggs hatch, the tiny spiders are called spiderlings.

△ Although it looks scary, this hairy Mexican tarantula is harmless to humans.

◁ A scorpion uses the poisonous sting at the end of its tail to stun insects and other prey.

Scorpions

There are almost 1000 kinds of scorpion. They live in deserts and other warm parts of the world. They avoid the heat of the day and come out to hunt at night.

◁ Garden spiders are common web-building spiders.

DID YOU KNOW?

Female scorpions give birth to live babies – then carry them on their back for two weeks.

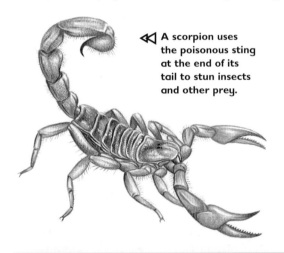

Spider's webs

Spiders spin webs in different shapes and patterns. Orb (round) webs are the most common. When an insect flies into the web, it gets stuck. The spider bites its prey – the bite contains venom (poison) that stops the prey from moving.

Orb-weaver spider ▷▷ spinning a web.

27

Insects

There are more insects than any other kind of animal. Scientists have named around one million kinds of insect so far, but there are probably more to discover.

Insects live almost everywhere – on high mountains, in hot deserts, and even in the sea!

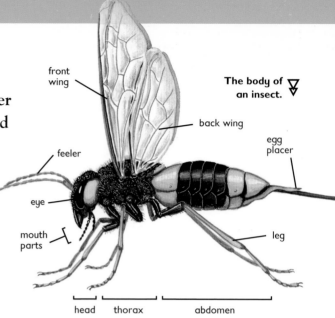

front wing

back wing

feeler

egg placer

eye

mouth parts

leg

The body of an insect.

head   thorax   abdomen

What is an insect?

Insects are animals without a backbone. Their bodies are protected inside a hard, waterproof case, called an exoskeleton.

An adult insect has three main body parts – its head, thorax and abdomen – and three pairs of legs. It also has wings.

Ladybirds are a kind of beetle. They feed on aphids, which are a kind of bug.

Beetles

Scientists split insects into groups. Beetles make up the biggest group, with over 400,000 kinds. Beetles come in many shapes, sizes and colours, but they all have thickened front wings. Many beetles help to break down dead plants and animals in the soil. Others hunt living insects.

Changing states

Most insects change shape as they grow up. Caterpillars make a total change to become butterflies. This is called complete metamorphosis.

Some insects only change a little to reach their adult form. Young grasshoppers gradually grow wings, for example. This is called incomplete metamorphosis.

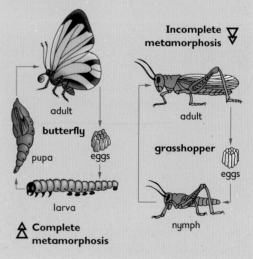

Incomplete metamorphosis

adult
butterfly
pupa
eggs
larva

Complete metamorphosis

adult
grasshopper
eggs
nymph

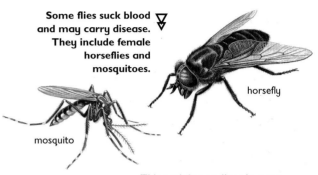

Flies

All flies have two pairs of wings, but the back ones are tiny. Flies only use their front wings for flying. Some flies do useful jobs, but others carry disease.

Some flies suck blood and may carry disease. They include female horseflies and mosquitoes.

horsefly

mosquito

△ A shield bug resting on a flower.

Bugs

Bugs are insects that cannot eat solid food. They use their needle-like beak to pierce a plant stem or an animal's skin – then suck up the juices inside!

Bees, wasps and ants

Bees, wasps and ants are close relatives. Many of them can sting. Some live in big groups called colonies. All the insects in a colony share the same mother – the queen.

▽ A caterpillar turns into a butterfly inside a case called a cocoon. This monarch butterfly is just coming out of its cocoon.

This social wasp lives in a papery nest with other wasps. ▽

Butterflies and moths

Butterflies and moths feed on nectar from flowers. Butterflies often have colourful wings and are active in the day. Moths often have dull wings and are active at night.

Other insects

There are many other kinds of insect. They include grasshoppers and crickets, fleas and lice, dragonflies, cockroaches and earwigs.

Fish

Fish are animals that live in the sea or in freshwater ponds and rivers. There are about 21,000 different kinds. They all have fins for swimming.

Fish also have gills – special flaps on either side of their head that allow them to breathe, or take in oxygen from the water.

Swimming

A fish has a smooth, streamlined shape so that it can glide through the water. It has strong muscles to move its body from side to side. It also has fins, to help it balance or slow down.

Inside its body, the fish has a little bag of air, called a swim bladder. This stops it from sinking in the water.

Baby fish

Most fish lay eggs – lots and lots of them! Fish that have just hatched are called fry. They have to look after themselves.

Fish senses

Just like you, a fish can see, hear, touch, smell and taste. Most fish have eyes on the sides of their heads, so they can see all around. Their ears are hidden inside their head.

Fish use smell to find their prey. They have taste buds in and around their mouths.

Special senses

Fish have nerves just under their skin that help them to work out what else is in the water. These nerves help fish to tell when there is a hunter nearby – or when there are animals that they can hunt!

FAST FACTS

Heaviest fish: Whale shark (40 tonnes)
Shortest fish: Pygmy goby (1 cm)
Fastest fish: Sailfish (109 km/h)

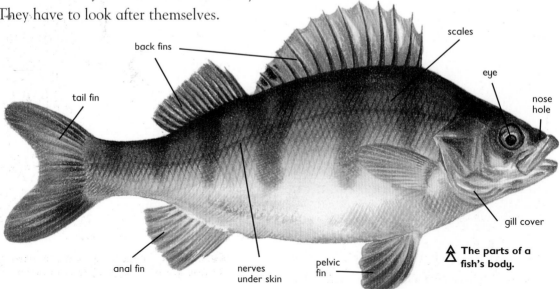

back fins

scales

tail fin

eye

nose hole

anal fin

nerves under skin

pelvic fin

gill cover

▲ The parts of a fish's body.

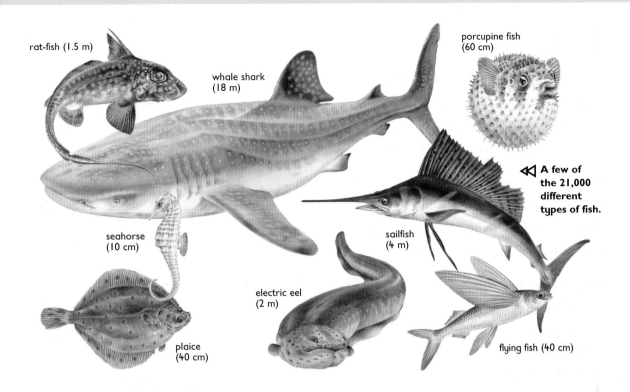

rat-fish (1.5 m)

whale shark
(18 m)

porcupine fish
(60 cm)

◁◁ **A few of
the 21,000
different
types of fish.**

seahorse
(10 cm)

sailfish
(4 m)

electric eel
(2 m)

plaice
(40 cm)

flying fish (40 cm)

Sharks, skates and rays

Sharks, skates and rays are a special group of fish. Their skeletons are made of a bendy material called cartilage, instead of bone. You have cartilage in your body – in your nose and your ears.

Most sharks, skates and rays are hunters. Skates and rays are flat-bodied fish that keep close to the sea-bed.

Blue-spotted fantail ray. ▷▷

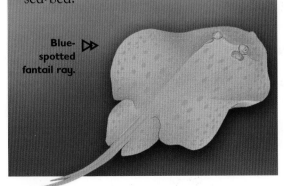

Fish food

Most fish in the oceans are hunters. They eat other fish, shellfish, squids or very tiny sea creatures called plankton. Fish that live in rivers and ponds also eat other animals, but some eat water plants instead.

A lion fish looks like it has a mane. This one is hunting a school (group) of cardinal fish.

Frogs and other amphibians

Frogs can live on land as well as in water. They belong to a family of animals called amphibians. Toads, newts, salamanders and blindworms are amphibians, too.

Amphibians all have moist, soft skins. They breathe partly through their skins.

The fire salamander's bright markings are a warning that its skin is poisonous.

There are over 300 kinds of newts and salamanders. This is a marbled newt.

Body temperature

Amphibians are cold-blooded animals. Their body temperature depends on the warmth of the air or water around them.

Kinds of amphibian

Frogs and toads are the most common amphibians. There are over 3500 kinds. They have strong back legs for jumping and swimming.

Newts and salamanders look like lizards, but with soft, slimy skin. Blindworms look like very big earthworms. Most are 30-70 cm long. They live in the tropics.

From tadpole to frog

Frogs lay their eggs in water. A young frog (tadpole) has a tail, and it breathes underwater with gills. As it grows, the tadpole's legs and lungs develop, and it can live on land. This body change is called metamorphosis.

A frog begins life as a tadpole, that hatches from an egg.

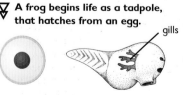   

gills

egg (spawn)   one day old   one month old   two months old   adult

Crocodiles, snakes and other reptiles

Crocodiles, snakes, lizards and tortoises are all reptiles. They have tough, dry, scaly skin and they lay eggs. Reptiles breathe through lungs, so the ones that live in rivers or the sea must come up to the surface for air.

Reptiles cannot make their own body heat. They have to bask in the sun to warm up.

▽ How long reptiles live.

Nile crocodile: 80 years

Giant tortoise: 150 years

Rat snake: 30 years

Iguana: 8 years

DID YOU KNOW?

Most Nile crocodiles live to about 80 years old, but some may live to be 200!

River reptiles

Crocodiles and alligators are fierce hunters that live in water. They mostly eat fish, but they sometimes kill and eat larger animals that come to the water to drink.

◁ Nile crocodiles sometimes eat zebras, wildebeest, young hippos – and even people.

◁ A cobra has poison fangs. Its bite may stop prey from moving, or even kill it.

Snakes and lizards

Snakes are hunters, too. They have no legs, so they slither or swim. Some snakes can kill an animal by curling around its body and squeezing tight.

Lizards are small reptiles. Many have colouring and markings that make them hard to see.

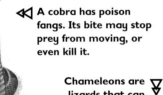

Chameleons are lizards that can change the colour of their skin to blend in with the background. ▽

Life in a shell

Tortoises and turtles have hard, horny shells. Tortoises live on land and eat plants. Turtles live in water. They eat seaweed and some sea creatures.

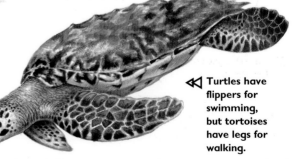

◁ Turtles have flippers for swimming, but tortoises have legs for walking.

Dinosaurs

Dinosaurs were reptiles that lived in prehistoric times. For 160 million years, they were the main group of animals on Earth. Dinosaurs died out 65 million years ago – more than 60 million years before the first human-like creatures lived.

The smallest dinosaurs were fast-moving and no bigger than chickens. The largest were slow plant-eaters, and also the biggest animals that have ever lived on land.

Early dinosaurs

The first dinosaurs lived over 220 million years ago in swamps and forests. They were quite small and ran on their back legs. Because they could stand on their back legs, they could reach higher for food.

Types of dinosaur

Over millions of years, all kinds of different dinosaurs appeared. Scientists split them into two groups – ones with hips like lizards and ones with hips like birds.

Warm-blooded or cold-blooded?

Today's reptiles are cold-blooded. They need heat from the Sun to become active. Scientists are not sure about the dinosaurs. Earth was warmer when they were alive. It would have been easier for large cold-blooded animals to stay active. Smaller dinosaurs might have been warm-blooded.

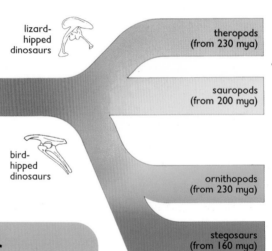

lizard-hipped dinosaurs

theropods
(from 230 mya)

sauropods
(from 200 mya)

bird-hipped dinosaurs

ornithopods
(from 230 mya)

stegosaurs
(from 160 mya)

ankylosaurs
(from 100 mya)

ceratopsians
(from 140 mya)

Different dinosaur groups and how many millions of years ago (mya) they appeared.

DID YOU KNOW?

The word dinosaur means 'terrible lizard'.

Teeth and food

Lizard-hipped dinosaurs had teeth at the front of their mouth. They could bite and tear, but not chew. All the meat-eaters were lizard-hipped. Bird-hipped dinosaurs had teeth at the back of their mouth. They could grind up plant stems and leaves. They were all plant-eaters.

Fearsome ▷▷ Tyrannosaurus rex was a meat-eater as tall as a two-storey building.

Triceratops

Some plant- ▷▷ eaters had armour to see off meat-eaters.

Scolosaurus

End of the dinosaurs

Around 65 million years ago, the dinosaurs suddenly died out. Some scientists think that a giant lump of space rock, called a meteorite, crashed into the Earth. It made a cloud of dust that blocked out the Sun and the Earth became too cold for dinosaurs.

▽ **Fossilized dinosaur footprints tell us how dinosaurs moved.**

Dinosaur fossils

We know about dinosaurs from fossils. Scientists piece together dinosaur bones to see how their bodies looked. When lots of bones are found together, scientists can guess that some dinosaurs might have lived in herds.

Dinosaur teeth tell us what dinosaurs ate, and dinosaur eggs tell us how dinosaurs had babies. There are lots of things fossils do not tell us, such as what colour dinosaurs were or what noises they made.

Birds

Birds are animals that have wings and feathers. Most birds can fly, but not all. Some can swim.

There are about 9000 different kinds of bird. The smallest would fit in the palm of your hand. The largest, the ostrich, grows taller than a person!

Where birds live

Birds live all over the world. Some live in gardens, cities and parks. Others live in rainforests, deserts, forests, or oceans. There are even birds in the icy wastes of the Arctic and Antarctic.

Wherever they live, birds make their own body heat using energy from food. This is called being warm-blooded.

Feathers

Birds are the only animals that have feathers. They have soft, downy feathers to keep them warm. They also have strong wing feathers. Outer feathers are waterproof, to keep off the rain.

Feathers are different colours. Many female birds are mainly brown so that they blend in with their surroundings. Male birds are often brightly coloured to attract a mate.

▽ A little owl in flight. Birds flap their wings to fly. They can also glide on the wind.

Migrating birds

Many birds move to a different part of the world for some months of the year. This is called migration. They spend the winter in warmer places where there is plenty of food. The Arctic tern flies as far as 35,000 km in a single year.

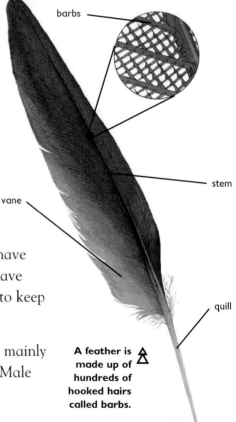

barbs

stem

vane

quill

A feather is made up of hundreds of hooked hairs called barbs.

DID YOU KNOW?

Birds don't have teeth. They gulp down their food whole. They swallow small stones that help to grind up the food inside their stomach.

Baby birds

Birds lay eggs, usually in a nest. Most parent birds sit on their eggs to keep them warm. After the eggs hatch, the parents feed the young chicks until they are old enough to find their own food.

◄◄ **The cuckoo lays its egg in another bird's nest – and the other bird raises its chick.**

Bird food

Bird beaks come in all different shapes. Sparrows have short, strong beaks for cracking seeds. Ducks have flat beaks for tugging up pondweed. Wading birds and seabirds have long, sharp beaks for spearing fish.

▽ **Wading birds live by the edges of rivers and lakes.**

curlew

pratincole

turnstone

avocet

phalarope

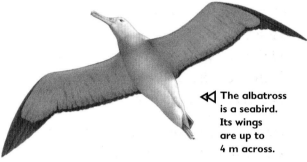

◄◄ **The albatross is a seabird. Its wings are up to 4 m across.**

Birds of prey

Eagles, falcons, hawks and kites are birds of prey. They hunt and kill other animals for food. They have big claws called talons for gripping their prey and hooked beaks for tearing flesh.

▽ **The red kite is a bird of prey. Its keen eyes can spot small animals down on the ground.**

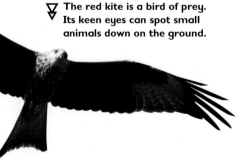

Bird song

Birds use calls and songs to talk to each other. Some songs attract a mate. There are also calls to warn that danger is coming or to keep a flock of birds close together.

▽ **Songbirds live all over the world.**

song thrush (Europe)

scarlet tanager (North America)

waxwing (Europe and North America)

Gouldian finch (Australia)

Mammals

Mammals are one of the main groups of animals. You are a mammal, and so are cats and dogs. Mammals range in size from enormous elephants and blue whales to tiny shrews.

There are about 4000 different kinds of mammal, and they live just about everywhere on Earth. Most live on land, but some live in the oceans.

Bats are the only mammals that can fly.

Mammal features

Mammals are warm-blooded, which means that they make their own body heat. They all have fur or hair at some stage in their lives. All female mammals feed their babies on milk.

Mammals are the only animals that have fur. This is an orang-utan.

Otters are excellent swimmers.

▽ Anteaters have no teeth. They use their sticky tongues to lick up insects.

What mammals eat

Some mammals eat only meat and some eat only plants. Other mammals eat a mix of plant and animal food. They are called omnivores. Hedgehogs, shrews and anteaters feed on insects. They are called insectivores.

Mammal babies

Most mammals give birth to live babies that develop inside the mother's body. Echidnas and duck-billed platypuses are different. These mammals lay eggs. But they still feed their babies on mother's milk.

Duck-billed platypus ▽

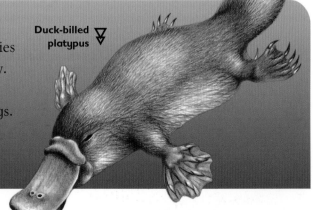

Kangaroos and other marsupials

Kangaroos are a special kind of mammal called a marsupial. Their babies develop inside a furry pouch on the mother's belly.

Koalas, opossums, wombats and wallabies are all marsupials too. Marsupials live only in Australia, New Guinea and the Americas.

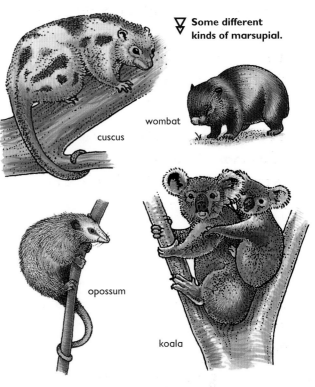

Some different kinds of marsupial.

cuscus

wombat

opossum

koala

Starting life

When baby marsupials are born, they are very tiny. Kangaroos are peanut-sized and some marsupials are the size of a grain of rice. Although they have hardly begun to develop, they have strong front legs and claws. They use these to crawl up to their mother's pouch.

DID YOU KNOW?

A group of kangaroos is called a mob.

Baby kangaroos, ▷▷ called joeys, stay in their mother's pouch until they are old enough to look after themselves.

Playing dead

The Virginia opossum plays a sneaky trick if it is frightened. To make its enemy go away, it pretends to be dead. The saying 'playing possum' means pretending to be dead.

Australian marsupials

The red kangaroo is the biggest marsupial. Like all kangaroos and wallabies, it has powerful back legs for jumping.

Koalas, wombats, possums and bandicoots also live in Australia. Koalas are picky eaters. They only eat the leaves of eucalyptus trees.

Meat-eating mammals

Cats are hunters. If a cat sees a bird on the ground it creeps towards the bird, keeping low and out of sight. If the cat gets close enough, it rushes out and pounces.

Pet cats are part of a group of mammals called carnivores. Any animal that eats other animals for food is a carnivore.

The tiger is a big cat that lives in Asia.

Cats

The cat family includes lions, tigers, cheetahs and jaguars. Like all hunters, cats have sharp senses. Their eyesight is excellent at night, which is when most cats hunt. Cats have good hearing, too.

A cat has two main weapons – its dagger-like front teeth and its razor-sharp claws. When its claws are not being used, the cat pulls them back into its paws, so that they stay sharp. Only the cheetah cannot do this.

A lion kills its prey with a bite to the throat that cuts off the animal's air supply.

A wolf hunts and lives in a pack.

Dogs

Pet dogs have many wild relatives. Wolves, coyotes and foxes all belong to the dog family. Dogs are hunters, but they are not as fussy as cats. Foxes, for instance, eat berries in the autumn, and will eat worms if they are hungry.

Dogs have good hearing and eyesight, but they rely most on smell. They find prey by following an animal's scent.

Bears

The bear family includes the world's biggest carnivore, the polar bear. Bears eat many plant foods, not just meat. Polar bears and brown bears are also skilled at catching fish in their enormous paws.

This brown bear and her ▷▷ cubs are fishing for salmon.

Scissor teeth

Carnivores can be large or small. They may live alone or in a group. The one thing they have in common is their teeth. All carnivores have four large scissor teeth which are perfect for slicing through flesh. As the mouth closes, the teeth slide past each other like blades.

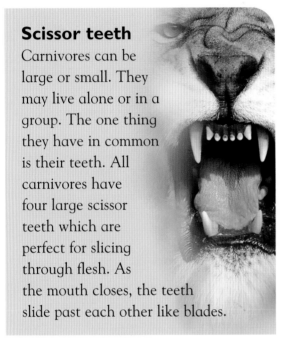

Other meat eaters

Not all carnivores are large animals. The smallest of all is the least weasel, which weighs less than two slices of bread. Other carnivores include hyenas, badgers, raccoons, skunks, polecats and meercats.

Hunting alone, a weasel catches mice, voles, rabbits and birds.

Hunters in danger

Pet cats and dogs are found in their millions all over the world, but their wild cousins are endangered. Some carnivores have been hunted by people, usually for their fur or because they might kill livestock. People have also destroyed the places where carnivores live, clearing the land for farmland or housing.

DID YOU KNOW?

Cheetahs are the fastest land animals, but only half of their chases end with a kill. African hunting dogs are the most successful carnivores. They kill seven out of every ten animals they hunt.

Top hunting ▷▷ speeds

Polar bear: 40 km/h

African hunting dog: 50 km/h

Cheetah: 100 km/h

Grazing mammals

Many mammals spend their lives eating grass. They include elephants, horses, cattle, deer and sheep.

Wild grazing mammals live on grassy plains, such as the prairies of North America or the African savannah. Tame grazing mammals are kept by farmers in most parts of the world.

Tame Asian elephants are sometimes trained to take part in processions.

Grassy diet

Plant-eaters are called herbivores. The main plant that grazing mammals eat is grass. It is not a high-energy food, so animals have to spend a lot of time eating.

Elephants, for example, eat for around 16 hours each day. Over half of their food is grass, but they also eat leaves, twigs and fruit.

DID YOU KNOW?

Grazing animals have special grinding teeth called molars at the back of their mouths. Molars help them to chew up grass and other plants.

The African elephant is the biggest grazing mammal – and the largest land animal.

Following food

Herds of grazing animals travel long distances to find fresh grass. Some make regular journeys. This is called migration. In Africa, wildebeest move to the savannah each November, at the start of the rainy season. In May, when the dry season begins, they move to the forests.

Elephants

There are two types of elephant, African elephants and Asian elephants. The Asian elephant has much smaller ears than the African elephant. Elephants use their long trunks to lift food into their mouth.

Like most grazers, elephants live in groups called herds. Some herds are enormous, and contain as many as 200 elephants.

Horses

Wild horses, such as zebras and wild asses, live in the grasslands of Africa and Asia. When they are in danger, they can run very fast over long distances to escape.

Most of the horses in the world are tame. In the past, horses pulled chariots and wagons. Today, they are used for riding or horse racing.

▽ Przewalski's horse is rare in the wild, but common in zoos.

Zebras are a kind of wild horse. △
They live in African grassland,
called savannah.

Other grazers

Cattle include cows and oxen, as well as bison, water buffalo, yaks and antelopes. All of these animals have horns and hoofed feet.

Deer have antlers instead of horns. Antlers are made of bone. The elk is the biggest kind of deer.

A male elk (or moose) ▽
uses its antlers to fight
other males.

▽ The gaur is a
wild ox that lives
in India and
South-east Asia.

Chewing the cud

Grass is hard to digest. Some grazers partly digest their food, then bring it back up to chew again. This is called chewing the cud. Animals that do this have special, four-part stomachs. Cows, goats, sheep, buffaloes and deer all chew the cud.

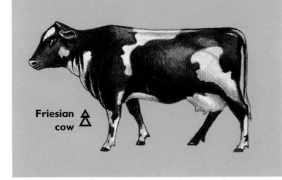

Friesian △
cow

Sea mammals

Whales, dolphins and seals live in the oceans. They may look like fish, but they are mammals, just like you.

Sea mammals give birth to live young and feed their babies on milk. They must also come up to the surface to breathe air.

Whales with teeth

There are two types of whale – toothed whales and baleen whales. Toothed whales include dolphins, porpoises and sperm whales. Dolphins and porpoises catch fish. Sperm whales feed mainly on squid.

Some different kinds of sea mammal. ▽

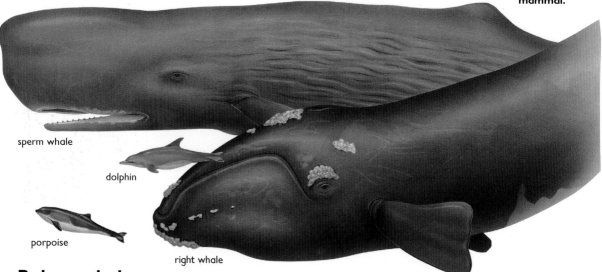

sperm whale

dolphin

porpoise

right whale

Baleen whales

Blue whales, right whales, grey whales and humpback whales are all baleen whales. Instead of teeth, they have huge, fringed plates made of baleen, a material similar to your fingernails. They use the plates to sift tiny animals called plankton out of the water.

Like all mammals, grey seals feed their young on milk. Seal babies are called pups. ▽

Other sea mammals

Seals, walruses and sea lions are also sea mammals. They are different to whales and dolphins, because they return to land to give birth. They use their flippers to move across the sand, rocks or ice.

Monkeys and apes

Monkeys and apes are primates – and so are you! All primates can grip things with their hands. Many can grip with their feet, too.

Compared to other animals, primates have a poor sense of smell. Sight is their most important sense. Primates can see colours.

◿◹ Gorillas are the biggest primates.

Apes

Gorillas, chimpanzees, orang-utans and gibbons are all apes. Apes are our closest animal relatives. They live for many years, have big brains and can walk upright. Like us, they do not have a tail.

◁◁ **Chimpanzees use tools. They dig insects from the ground with a stick.**

What primates eat

Some primates eat insects, but most feed on fruit or leaves. Some apes also eat meat. Male chimpanzees sometimes hunt together in groups.

Monkeys

Monkeys are similar to apes, but usually smaller. Most monkeys have tails. A few live on the ground, but most jump or swing through the trees. South American monkeys have tails that can grip, which they use like an extra arm.

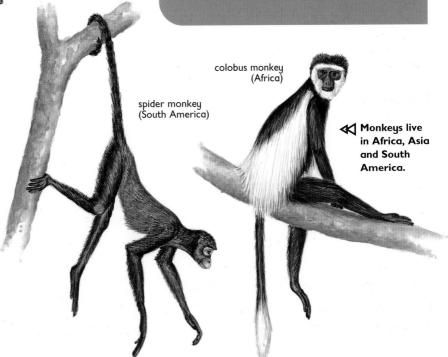

spider monkey
(South America)

colobus monkey
(Africa)

◁◁ **Monkeys live in Africa, Asia and South America.**

45

Animals in danger

Imagine a world with no turtles, tigers or toucans. Large numbers of animals are dying out in the wild. Some animals disappear before we even discover them.

With humans wanting more space for houses, factories and farms, there is less space for other living things.

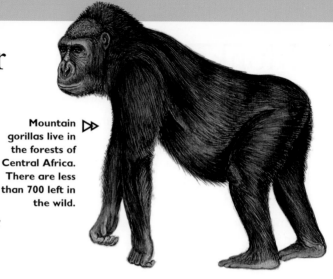

Mountain ▶▶ gorillas live in the forests of Central Africa. There are less than 700 left in the wild.

Animal homes

The biggest threat is when animals lose their habitat (the place where they live). People clear land to build on, or to grow crops and raise animals. They cut down forests for their timber (wood). They also drain marshes and clear grasslands.

Another problem is pollution. This is when poisons from towns, farms and factories get into the land or the sea.

Hunting and fishing

Animals have also become rare because people hunt them. Some people shoot animals for sport. People also kill animals for their skin, feathers or fur. Elephants and rhinos are hunted for their tusks and horns.

Some endangered animals, including gorillas and whales, are killed for their meat. Fishing boats sometimes catch endangered fish and other sea life in their nets. Nets can damage the sea-bed, too.

DID YOU KNOW?

Every minute people cut or burn down an area of rainforest the size of 20 football pitches.

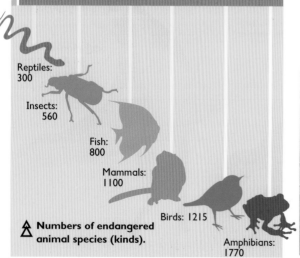

Reptiles: 300

Insects: 560

Fish: 800

Mammals: 1100

Birds: 1215

Amphibians: 1770

▲ Numbers of endangered animal species (kinds).

These people from Greenpeace are trying to stop a fishing trawler from dropping its nets. ▽▽

Pets

Wild animals are also caught to be sold as pets. Some people will pay a lot of money to own a rare snake, bird, monkey or wild cat. Others collect butterflies, beetles, or birds' eggs. Collecting rare animals is against the law, but it still happens because it is hard to catch the people involved.

Other animals

Sometimes, people bring new animals into an area and this can cause a problem for the animals that already live there. The new animals might hunt them, eat up all their food or carry disease. This is not such a problem now, because there is not much land left to discover.

Dead as a dodo

The dodo was a large bird that lived on the island of Mauritius in the Indian Ocean. It could not fly and it built its nest on the ground. In the 1500s, Dutch settlers brought dogs, pigs and rats to the island. These animals killed the birds and stole their eggs. By 1700, the dodo was extinct.

Spix's macaw is extinct in the wild but zoos are breeding the bird.

Some extinct ▷▷ animals.

moa

dodo

Tasmanian wolf

quagga

Saving animals

Governments have passed laws to stop animals being killed and they have set up nature reserves and national parks.

Many people care about wildlife and fight to protect it. Groups such as the WWF (formerly known as the World

Wildlife Fund), Friends of the Earth and Greenpeace work to protect endangered animals and their habitats.

Zoos also work hard to help rare animals. Sometimes, animals bred in zoos can be put back into the wild.

The WWF is a group ▷▷ that fights to protect animals. Their symbol is the panda, an endangered animal from China.

WWF®

for a living planet®

Earth

The Earth is the planet that we live on. It travels around the Sun in our Solar System. So far as we know, Earth is the only planet with living things on it.

Two-thirds of Earth's surface is water and one third is land. Earth is surrounded by an atmosphere – layers of air that contain oxygen.

On the move

Like all the planets, the Earth is constantly moving. It spins around its axis (an imaginary line that passes between the poles). The Earth also travels in a path, called an orbit, around the Sun.

It takes one day for the Earth to spin around its axis. It takes one year for the Earth to orbit the Sun.

△ From space, you can see Earth's oceans, land and ice-covered poles. You can also see the swirling clouds.

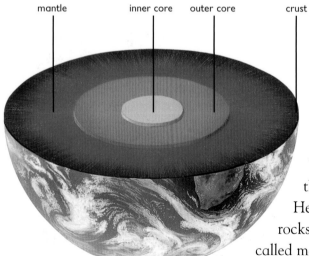

mantle　　inner core　　outer core　　crust

The Earth is made △ up of three main layers – the crust, mantle and core.

Earth's crust

The outer layer of the Earth is called the crust. It includes the oceans and the land where we live. It is made of hard rock, broken up into several huge pieces, called plates.

Earth's mantle

The layer beneath the Earth's crust, called the mantle, is around 2900 kilometres thick. Heat from inside the Earth makes some of the rocks in the mantle melt. The hot, liquid rock is called magma.

Earth's core

The centre of the Earth is called its core. The outer core is made of liquid metals. The inner core is solid metal. The temperature in the core is around 5000 °C.

How the Earth and Moon formed

1. Around 4.5 billion years ago, material in a huge spinning cloud of gas clumped together. The clumps became the Sun and planets, including Earth.

2. When it was first formed, Earth was a ball of molten rock.

3. Before the Earth cooled, it was hit by a giant meteorite (a rock hurtling through space).

4. A huge piece of the Earth split off and became the Moon.

Continental plates

The Earth's crust is less than 50 kilometres thick in most places. It is broken up into large pieces, called continental plates. These float on the hot, molten rock underneath them.

Moving plates

Continental plates move very slowly – about 2.5 centimetres a year. Where plates crash, the edges buckle and mountains form. Earthquakes and volcanoes also happen at the borders between plates.

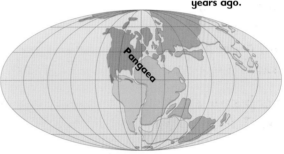

▽ Earth's continental plates 250 million years ago.

Pangaea

Laurasia

Gondwanaland

△ Earth's continental plates 175 million years ago.

FAST FACTS ▷▷

The sizes of Earth's continents

Africa	30,319,000 sq km
Antarctica	13,209,000 sq km
Asia	44,387,000 sq km
Europe	10,531,000 sq km
North America	24,249,000 sq km
Oceania	8,510,000 sq km
South America	17,832,000 sq km

▽ Earth's continental plates today.

plate boundaries
—— moving apart
---- moving together
—— passive

EURASIAN
HELLENIC
IRANIAN
ARABIAN
PHILIPPINE
NORTH AMERICAN
JUAN DE FUCA
NORTH AMERICAN
CARIBBEAN
COCOS
PACIFIC
AFRICAN
INDIAN
NASCA
SOUTH AMERICAN
ANTARCTIC
ANTARCTIC

DID YOU KNOW?

Today, the land on Earth is split into seven continents. Millions of years ago it made up one enormous supercontinent, called Pangaea.

Climate and weather

Wind, rain, clouds and sun – they are all part of the weather. Weather is what is happening in the atmosphere around you. It can change very quickly.

Climate is not the same thing as weather. Climate means the average weather in a place over a long time.

Winds

All weather happens because heat from the Sun warms the surface of the Earth. This warming keeps the air in the atmosphere on the move as wind.

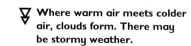

Where warm air meets colder air, clouds form. There may be stormy weather.

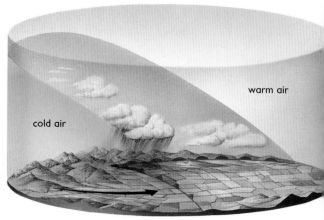

warm air

cold air

A hurricane seen from space. Hurricanes are violent storms, with winds that blow at up to 300 km/h.

Rain and the water cycle

As the Sun warms Earth's oceans, rivers and lakes, it turns surface water into a gas – water vapour. This rises and forms clouds.

When the clouds cool, the water falls to Earth as rain or snow. Rain fills Earth's oceans, rivers and lakes. Here, it is heated by the Sun and the water cycle begins again.

Water goes round and round in a process called the water cycle.

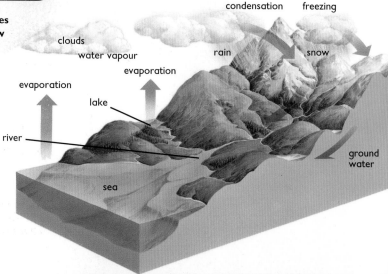

condensation   freezing

clouds
water vapour   rain   snow

evaporation

evaporation

lake

river

sea

ground water

FAST FACTS ▶▶

Hottest place: *Dalliol, Ethiopia (average 34.4°C)*
Coldest place: *Plateau Station, Antarctica (average -56.6°C)*
Driest place: *Atacama Desert, Chile*
Rainiest place: *Mount Waialeale, Hawaii (350 days per year)*
Windiest place: *Commonwealth Bay, Antarctica (gales of 320 km/h)*

The Equator and climate

Places near the Equator receive the most sun, so they usually have hot weather. Their climate, or average weather, is tropical, which means it is warm all year, often with a dry and a rainy season.

At the North and South Poles, far from the Equator, there is a cold, polar climate. Summers are short and winters are long and dark.

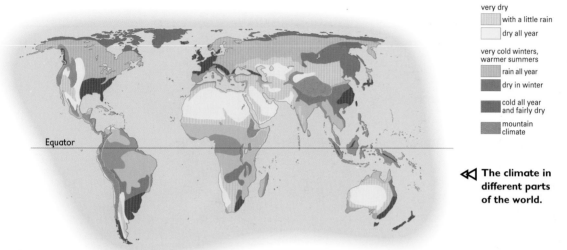

warm summers, mild winters
- dry in summer
- dry in winter
- rain all year

very warm all year and very rainy
- rain all year
- dry in winter

very dry
- with a little rain
- dry all year

very cold winters, warmer summers
- rain all year
- dry in winter

- cold all year and fairly dry
- mountain climate

◁◁ The climate in different parts of the world.

The seasons

During the year, the seasons change. From March to September, the North Pole tilts towards the Sun. Places in the northern half of the Earth have more sunshine and warmer weather.

From September to March, the South Pole tilts towards the Sun. Places in the southern half of the Earth have warmer weather.

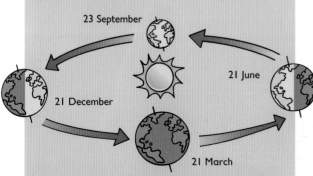

◁◁ Earth takes one year to travel round the Sun. The seasons change as different parts get more sunshine.

Mountains, oceans and climate

How high up a place is affects its climate. The higher you go, the cooler it becomes. Mount Kilimanjaro is in tropical Africa, but it has snow all year round.

Places by the sea usually have milder winters and cooler summers than places inland. This is because the sea warms up and cools down more quickly than land.

Winds and climate

Winds affect climate, too. In the Sahara Desert, the winds are hot and very dry, so there is little rainfall. But winds that blow from the sea, such as the monsoon winds in South-east Asia, bring lots of rain.

Volcanoes and earthquakes

Hot lava, ash and smoke pouring out of volcanoes cause damage in many parts of the world. The shaking of the ground in an earthquake can destroy cities.

Both earthquakes and volcanoes happen because of movements in the surface, or crust, of the Earth.

A volcano erupts

Earth's crust is made up of moving plates that float on a layer of hot, molten rock (magma). Volcanoes happen when magma pushes up through cracks. An erupting volcano sends out molten rock (lava) and clouds of ash and gases.

Building up

As lava cools, it hardens into solid rock. Over time, lava layers build up into a mountain shape.

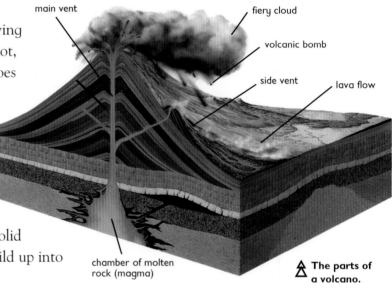

main vent · fiery cloud · volcanic bomb · side vent · lava flow · chamber of molten rock (magma)

The parts of a volcano.

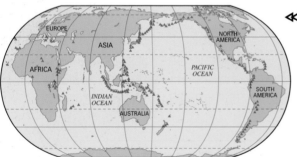

EUROPE · ASIA · NORTH AMERICA · AFRICA · PACIFIC OCEAN · INDIAN OCEAN · AUSTRALIA · SOUTH AMERICA

A map of the world's active volcanoes. There are so many around the edge of the Pacific Ocean plate that the area is called the 'ring of fire'.

Damage from an earthquake in the Japanese city of Kobe in 1995.

Earthquakes

Strong earthquakes usually happen when two plates rub against each other. They are common in places such as Japan and California, which are at the edges of plates.

Mountains

Mountains are high peaks of land. They are formed by movements of the Earth's surface, and they are shaped by rain, sun, ice and wind.

Mountains are harsh places to live, because temperatures are low and the air is thin. Some people climb mountains for sport or to enjoy the beautiful scenery.

Fold mountains

Fold mountains form when two pieces of the Earth's crust slowly crash into each other. Over millions of years, the rocks of the crust are pushed upwards to form mountains.

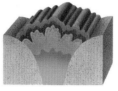

⚠ **Fold mountain.**

Block mountains

Block mountains form when huge blocks of rock are tilted or lifted up along lines of weakness, called faults.

⚠ **Block mountain.**

Dome mountains

Dome mountains form when molten rock pushing up from below meets strong rocks at the surface. The rocks bulge to form a dome.

⚠ **Dome mountain.**

Shaping mountains

Valleys form when rivers or glaciers (rivers of ice) wear away the softer rocks and carve deep channels in the mountainside.

Mountains are also worn away by rain and wind. The oldest mountains have rounded tops and gentle slopes.

▽ **A valley in the Swiss Alps, Europe.**

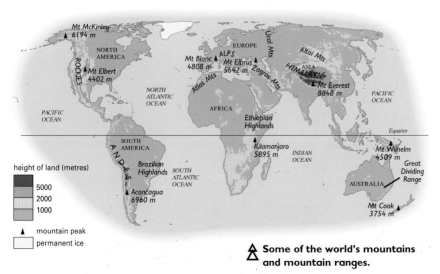

Mt McKinley 6194 m
NORTH AMERICA
ROCKIES
Mt Elbert 4402 m
NORTH ATLANTIC OCEAN
PACIFIC OCEAN
EUROPE
Mt Blanc 4808 m
ALPS
Atlas Mts
Mt Elbrus 5642 m
Ural Mts
Zagros Mts
Altai Mts
ASIA
HIMALAYAS
Mt Everest 8848 m
PACIFIC OCEAN
AFRICA
Ethiopian Highlands
Equator
SOUTH AMERICA
ANDES
Brazilian Highlands
SOUTH ATLANTIC OCEAN
Kilamanjaro 5895 m
INDIAN OCEAN
Mt Wilhelm 4509 m
Great Dividing Range
AUSTRALIA
Aconcagua 6960 m
Mt Cook 3754 m

height of land (metres)
5000
2000
1000

▲ mountain peak
permanent ice

⚠ **Some of the world's mountains and mountain ranges.**

Rocks and minerals

Rocks are all around you. You see them in cliffs, along the seashore and in the ground. Rocks are the hard, solid parts of the Earth.

All rocks are made up of substances called minerals. If you look closely at a rock you can see the different minerals in it.

Cliffs made of sedimentary rocks. You can see how the rock built up in layers. △

Minerals

There are more than 2500 kinds of mineral. Scientists can tell each one by its colour, hardness, crystal shape and the way it reflects light.

Gold, silver, diamonds and rubies are minerals. So are the clays used to make pottery and the graphite in your pencil lead.

chalcopyrite

azurite

△ Both of these minerals contain the metal, copper. It gives them their blue colour.

Rock types

There are three main types of rock. Igneous rocks form when hot, molten rock cools and becomes solid. Basalt and granite are igneous rocks.

Sedimentary rocks form when mud, sand or broken rock builds up. Sandstone, shale and limestone are sedimentary rocks.

Sometimes igneous or sedimentary rocks heat up under great pressure. They change into a new type of rock – metamorphic rock. Marble and slate are metamorphic rocks.

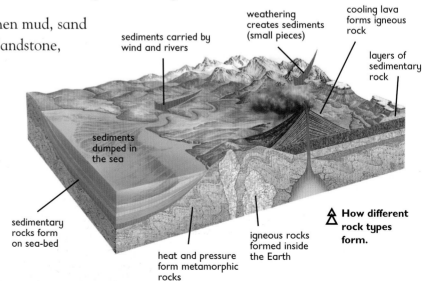

weathering creates sediments (small pieces)

cooling lava forms igneous rock

sediments carried by wind and rivers

layers of sedimentary rock

sediments dumped in the sea

sedimentary rocks form on sea-bed

heat and pressure form metamorphic rocks

igneous rocks formed inside the Earth

△ How different rock types form.

Shaping the landscape

The rocky surface of the Earth is being slowly worn away by water, ice, wind and sun. This is called erosion.

Erosion breaks down rocks into tiny pieces that wash away. Without erosion, there would be no cliffs to walk along or caves to explore.

Weathering

The breaking down of rocks by snow and frost, sun and rain is called weathering. Rainwater can dissolve some kinds of rock, such as limestone. If rain seeps underground, it can create underground holes and caves.

Water wears away rock when it turns into ice, too. Water collects in tiny cracks in rocks. When the water freezes, it pushes the cracks wider because ice takes up more space than water.

△ The wind shaped these sandstone rocks in Utah, USA.

scree (rock pieces)

△ Ice has made these rocks jagged. It pushed open big cracks in the rock.

The sea

Pounding sea waves wear away coastlines and create cliffs and sea caves. Waves may also build up coasts. They wash up sand and pieces of rock to form beaches.

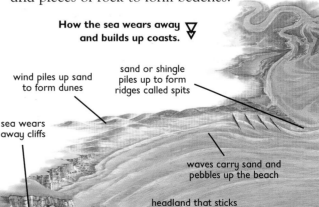

▽ How the sea wears away
▽ and builds up coasts.

wind piles up sand to form dunes

sand or shingle piles up to form ridges called spits

sea wears away cliffs

waves carry sand and pebbles up the beach

headland that sticks out into the sea is slowly worn away

Deserts

Deserts are the driest places on Earth. They have less than 250 millimetres of rain each year.

Most deserts are hot because they are near the tropics. But some deserts are extremely cold because they are near the poles.

Desert landscape

Most deserts are lands of sand and rock. The wind blows the sand into hills called dunes. The dunes are constantly moving.

An oasis is a place in the desert where there is water at the surface. Palm trees and other plants may grow there.

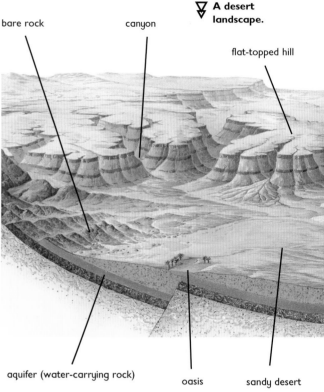

A desert landscape.

bare rock

canyon

flat-topped hill

aquifer (water-carrying rock)

oasis

sandy desert

Desert life

Plants and animals have to be tough to survive desert conditions. Desert plants often store water in their stems, leaves or roots. Desert animals may look for food at night, when it is cooler.

Many desert peoples are nomads, which means they move from place to place. They live in tents and keep animals, such as goats and camels.

Camels carry people and goods across deserts. They can survive for weeks without a drink.

FAST FACTS

Largest hot desert: Sahara (8.4 million sq km)
Highest temperature: 58 °C (Libya, 1922)
Longest drought: 400 years (Atacama Desert, Chile)
Highest dunes: 430 m high (eastern Algeria)

A gemsbok in the Namib Desert, Africa. The gemsbok is a kind of antelope that grazes on desert plants.

Forests

Forests are places where the land is covered with trees. About a fifth of the Earth is forest. Different kinds grow in different climates.

Forests are important habitats for animals and plants. They also provide people with useful products such as wood, paper, food and dyes.

△ Deciduous trees drop their leaves for winter or for the dry season. Leaves lose their green colour before they fall and change to red, yellow and orange.

▽ Part of a South American rainforest. There are different layers of plant and animal life.

1 harpy eagle
2 macaw
3 spider monkey
4 cock of the rock
5 tree boa
6 sloth
7 ocelot
8 tree frog
9 capybara
10 coral snake

canopy

understorey

forest floor

Rainforests

Rainforests grow where the weather is hot and wet all year round. They are home to hundreds of kinds of tree, as well as many other plants. Most are evergreen, so they give rainforest animals food and shelter all year round.

Broad-leaved forests

Broad-leaved forests grow where it is cool in winter and warm in summer. Most of the trees are deciduous, which means that they lose their leaves in winter.

DID YOU KNOW?

Like all green plants, forest trees release oxygen into the atmosphere. Without them, you would not have any oxygen to breathe.

▽ Forests are disappearing. They are cut down for their wood, or to make space for farms or housing.

Coniferous forests

Coniferous forests grow in cold climates. The main trees are conifers (cone-bearing trees), such as pines. Most conifers are evergreen. Their pyramid shape and needle-like leaves help any snow to slip off.

Grasslands

Grasslands include the prairies of North America, steppes of central Asia and the African savannah. They cover more than a fifth of the Earth.

Grass is an important food for many animals. People use grasslands to graze their animals. They also grow grasses to eat, such as wheat and rice.

African grasslands, called savannah, are home to herds of elephants, zebra and wildebeest.

Grassland animals

Grasslands are home to grazing animals and also the meat-eaters that feed on them. Grazing animals that live in East Africa's savannah include giraffes, elephants, rhinos, gazelles and zebras. Hunters include big cats.

FAST FACTS

- meadows (western Europe)
- pampas (South America)
- prairie (North America)
- savannah (East Africa)
- steppes (central Europe and Asia)
- veld (southern Africa)

People and grasslands

Humans have changed grasslands. Some grassland animals were hunted too much in the past, so now there are not many left. Large areas of grassland have been ploughed up so that farmers can grow grass crops. Other areas, such as the pampas, are used for grazing cattle.

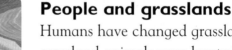

◀◀ In North America, large areas of the prairie are now farmland. Grass crops, such as this barley, grow there.

Rivers and lakes

When rain falls or snow melts, trickles of water run off the land. Sometimes the trickles join to form small streams, which join to form a river.

Sometimes the water collects in a hollow – this is called a lake.

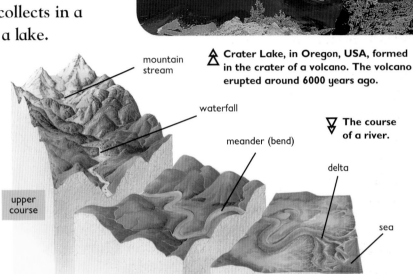

△ Crater Lake, in Oregon, USA, formed in the crater of a volcano. The volcano erupted around 6000 years ago.

Along the river

Near its source, a river is small but fast-flowing. Further along, it flows more slowly. Near its mouth (where it meets the sea), the river dumps mud that it has been carrying. This builds a delta – a fan shape of islands and channels.

mountain stream

waterfall

▽ The course of a river.

meander (bend)

delta

upper course

sea

middle course

lower course

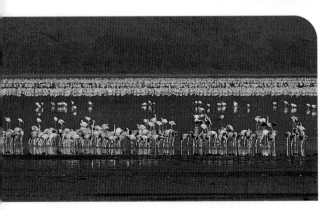

Rivers, lakes and people

Rivers and lakes give people water for drinking, washing and watering fields. They are a transport route for boats. People can also build dams that use the power of flowing water to create electricity.

Freshwater life

Rivers and lakes are a habitat for many kinds of plants. Some live on the banks, some on the surface and some under the water. Freshwater animals include insects, frogs, fish and birds.

◁◁ Lesser flamingos on Lake Nakuru, a salty lake in Kenya.

FAST FACTS ▷▷

Longest river: Nile, Africa (6673 km)
Largest freshwater lake: Lake Superior, Canada/USA (83,270 sq km)
Deepest lake: Lake Baykal, Russia (1741 m)
Highest waterfall: Angel Falls, Venezuela (979 m)

Oceans and seas

The Earth is a watery planet. Seas and oceans cover more than two-thirds of its surface. There are five oceans – the Pacific, Atlantic, Indian, Arctic and Southern Oceans.

Most seas are parts of oceans, but some are surrounded by land.

 The oceans of the world.

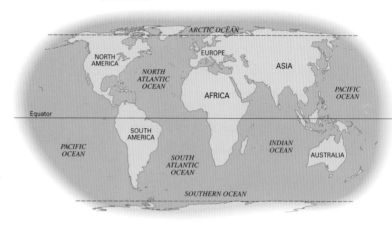

When the wind blows across the ocean, it whips up ripples of water called waves.

Wind and waves

The water in the oceans is always on the move. The wind creates waves, but these only stir up the surface. The ocean water itself is moved by currents and tides.

Currents and tides

Ocean currents are bodies of water that are constantly moving. Some flow deep along the sea floor. Others flow near the surface.

Tides are the rise and fall of the oceans. They happen because of the pull of a force called gravity. The Moon's gravity tugs at the Earth as the Earth spins in space.

The ocean floor

The bottom of the sea contains mountains and valleys, just like the land. The mountain chains are called mid-ocean ridges. Some mountains are so tall that they break through the surface as islands. The valleys are called trenches.

The sea-bed. ▷▷

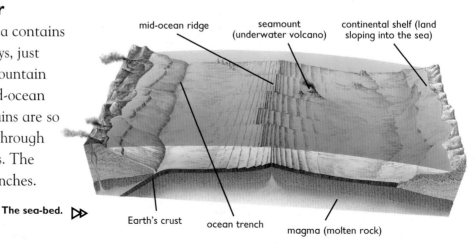

mid-ocean ridge

seamount (underwater volcano)

continental shelf (land sloping into the sea)

Earth's crust

ocean trench

magma (molten rock)

△ **Coral comes in many different shapes and colours.**
△ **Reef fish are colourful, too, with amazing patterns.**

Life out at sea

Some types of fish and a few large mammals, such as whales and dolphins, live in the middle of the oceans. They feed on fish or tiny plants and animals called plankton.

The size of the world's oceans. ▽

million sq km

180					
150	166,240,000				
120		86,560,000	73,430,000		
90					
60					
30				20,330,000	13,220,000
0					
	Pacific	Atlantic	Indian	Southern	Arctic

DID YOU KNOW?

The Pacific is the world's largest ocean. It covers more of the Earth's surface than all of the land put together.

Life near the shore

Most of the animals and plants in the ocean live near the coast. Coral reefs grow near coasts in the warmest parts of the world. Coral is built up from millions of dead and living animals. Tropical fish, tiger sharks and giant clams live on coral reefs.

◁◁ **Plankton are tiny animals and plants that float near the surface of the ocean. Many animals live by feeding on plankton.**

Life in the deep

The deeper you go, the less life there is in the ocean. Below 200 metres, there is not much light, so there are no plants and fewer animals. Even fewer live in the cold, dark waters below 1000 metres.

People and oceans

People harvest fish, shellfish and seaweed from the oceans. They drill the sea-bed for oil and gas. Seas provide salt and cement. Oceans are also used for transporting goods and people in ships.

▽ **Different kinds of plants and animals live at different levels of a rocky shore.**

Seashore

The seashore is the part of the coast where the ocean or sea meets the land. Rocky shores have rock pools full of plants and animals. On sandy or muddy shores, animals hide beneath the surface. There may be as many as 100,000 animals per square metre.

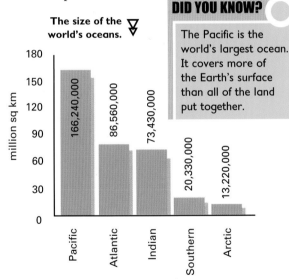

1 sea kelp
2 serrated wrack
3 sea anemone
4 thong weed
5 starfish
6 bladder wrack
7 mussels
8 knotted wrack
9 barnacles
10 spiral wrack
11 channel wrack
12 lichen

Pollution

People cause pollution when they damage their surroundings. Pollution includes litter, and waste from factories, farms and cars.

There are laws to control pollution and groups that work to look after the environment. However, pollution is still a big problem.

In some big cities, the air is so polluted that people wear masks. The masks stop them from breathing in dust, soot and chemicals.

A photo taken from space, showing the hole in the ozone layer above Antarctica. The red and grey areas contain no ozone.

The ozone layer

Ozone is a gas that surrounds the world, and protects Earth from the harmful rays in sunlight. However, pollution is destroying the ozone layer. Without the protection of the ozone layer, more people will get skin cancer.

Air pollution

Burning fuels, such as coal, oil and petrol, produces waste gases. Factories, power stations and traffic all burn fuels and make waste gases, which get into the air. Polluted air harms people's lungs.

Acid rain

When waste gases mix with water in the atmosphere, they can form acid rain. Acid rain damages trees and buildings. When it falls into lakes and rivers, it can kill fish and other wildlife.

Greenhouse gases

Some of the gases in the atmosphere act like the glass in a greenhouse, trapping heat from the Sun. Carbon dioxide is the main greenhouse gas.

People are putting more carbon dioxide into the air. It is released from car exhausts and power stations. Many scientists say these extra greenhouse gases are making the world warmer. This is called global warming.

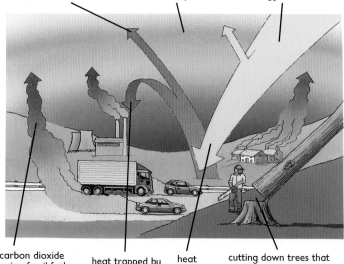

Causes of greenhouse gases.

heat energy escapes into space

energy reflected off the atmosphere

energy from Sun

extra carbon dioxide from burning fossil fuels

heat trapped by greenhouse gases

heat

cutting down trees that absorb carbon dioxide

DID YOU KNOW?

In 2002 the oil tanker *Prestige* sank off the coast of Spain. Over the following months, it leaked more than 60,000 tonnes of oil.

Water pollution

There are many kinds of water pollution. It includes waste from factories, sewage from people's homes and oil from tankers or pipelines.

Some pollution comes from the land. Many farmers use chemicals to improve their soil and to kill insect pests. These chemicals wash into rivers when there has been heavy rain. They can kill river wildlife.

Rubbish

People cause pollution when they dump their rubbish. Some rubbish rots away quite quickly, but many plastics will never decay.

Rubbish left by ▷▷ tourists in Nepal. Litter is ruining some of the most beautiful places on the planet.

Nuclear waste

Waste from nuclear power stations is another kind of pollution. Nearly all nuclear waste is safely contained, but small amounts do sometimes escape. Nuclear waste can stay radioactive, or carry on giving out dangerous rays, for thousands of years.

Pollution and the future

Scientists around the world are looking for ways to stop the damage caused by pollution. Governments have passed laws to control it. Everyone can play a part, by recycling and by using energy wisely.

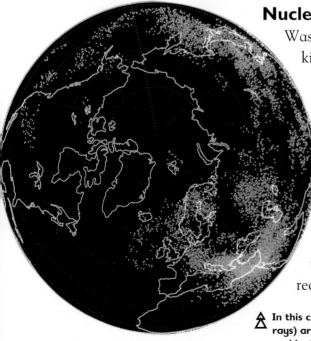

In this computer picture, areas of radioactivity (dangerous rays) are pink. It shows how nuclear waste spread after an accident in 1986 at Chernobyl power station (now in Ukraine).

Astronomy

Look at the lights in the night sky. A few are planets, many are stars, and some are huge galaxies, each one full of billions of stars.

Astronomy is the study of the planets, stars and galaxies that make up our vast Universe.

A closer look

Early astronomers had only their eyes to watch the sky. When telescopes were invented in 1608, astronomers were able to see the stars more clearly. Galileo Galilei was one of the first astronomers to use a telescope.

Constellations

When you look up at the stars, they seem to make patterns or pictures. These groups of stars are called constellations. Star charts show the constellations.

DID YOU KNOW?

The stars in a constellation look close together. Really they are millions of kilometres apart.

This star chart shows the constellations you can see from the northern half of the world.

This star chart shows the constellations you can see from the southern half of the world.

An observatory is a place where astronomers study the sky. Many are built on mountain tops, where they will get the clearest view.

You can study the night sky with a telescope, binoculars – or just your own eyes!

Telescopes

Some telescopes collect the faint light from distant objects. Some measure other rays from stars and galaxies, such as X-rays or radio waves. Most telescopes are on Earth, but some, like the Hubble Space Telescope, are up in space.

Sun

The Sun is our nearest and our most important star. Like all stars, the Sun is a giant ball of hot gas.

Without the Sun, there would be no life on Earth. The Sun provides us with heat and light.

Burning ball

The energy that makes the Sun shine is made in the Sun's core or centre. Temperatures there reach 16 million °C. In the intense heat, atoms of hydrogen gas join together, releasing huge amounts of energy.

The Sun's surface

At the surface of the Sun temperatures are around 6000 °C. In some places, cooler, darker patches called sunspots appear. These come and go in an 11-year cycle.

Jets of hot gas shoot out from the surface of the Sun and then fall back again.

DID YOU KNOW?

The Sun is only halfway through its life, but it is already 5000 million years old.

Solar eclipse

Sometimes the Moon lines up between the Earth and the Sun, and blocks out the sunlight. This is called a solar eclipse. During a total solar eclipse you can see the faint ring of gases around the Sun.

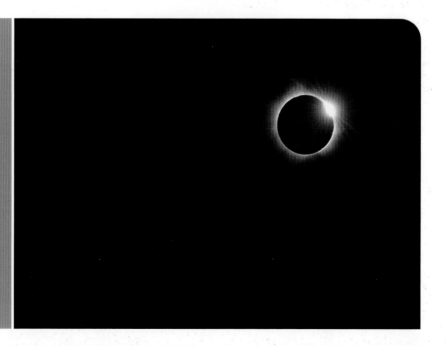

Moon

The Moon is the Earth's closest neighbour in space. It is the only other world that people have visited.

The Moon is not a planet. It is a natural satellite of the Earth. A satellite is something that travels around a planet.

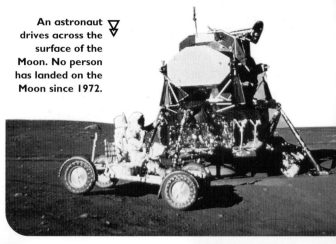

An astronaut drives across the surface of the Moon. No person has landed on the Moon since 1972.

Full Moon

New Moon

The phases of the Moon.

◀◀ The Moon's rocky surface is covered with craters.

DID YOU KNOW?

After the Sun, the Moon is the brightest object in the sky. It does not give out its own light. It shines because it reflects the light of the Sun.

Lunar landscape

The Moon's surface is covered with craters. Many are over 100 kilometres across. The craters were made when giant lumps of space rock, called meteorites, crashed into the Moon.

Phases of the Moon

The Moon circles the Earth, while the Earth goes round the Sun. It takes about a month for the Moon to travel around the Earth. During this time it changes from a Full Moon to a New Moon and back again. These different shapes are called the phases of the Moon.

Solar System

The Solar System is made up of the Sun and all the things that travel around it. Solar means 'of the Sun'.

The Solar System is so big that it is hard to imagine. But compared to the rest of the Universe, it is just a tiny speck.

Planets and years

The time it takes a planet to go round the Sun is equal to one year on that planet. It takes around 365 Earth days for the Earth to go around the Sun.

A year on Mercury, the planet nearest the Sun, is just 88 Earth days.

A year on Neptune, the planet furthest from the Sun, is more than 60,000 Earth days.

▽ The planets and their orbits (paths around the Sun).

Our star

The Sun is the largest body in the Solar System. Like all stars, it gives off huge amounts of heat and light.

The Sun produces a strong pulling force called gravity. The pull of gravity stops all the planets from flying off into outer space.

The planets

Eight planets orbit (travel around) the Sun. Mercury is the nearest to the Sun and Neptune is furthest away. Space probes have visited all the planets.

△ *Sojourner* landed on Mars in 1997 and photographed its surface. Space probes and robot landers find out about the planets.

The Solar System's eight planets. They are drawn to scale so that you can compare their sizes. ▽

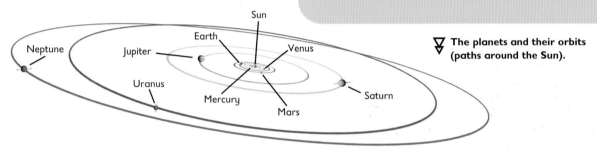

Rock, gas and ice

Mercury, Venus, Earth and Mars are small, rocky planets. Jupiter and Saturn are giant balls of gas. Uranus and Neptune are large planets made of gas and ice.

Moons

Moons are natural satellites – things that travel round planets. All the planets except Mercury and Venus have moons. The Earth's Moon is one of the biggest – only Jupiter and Saturn have bigger moons.

The surface of Venus is always hidden by thick cloud. This image was taken using radar, which passes through the cloud.

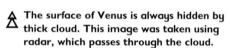

FAST FACTS

Biggest planet:	Jupiter (142,980 km across)
Smallest planet:	Mercury (4879 km across)
Most moons:	Jupiter (over 60)
Least moons:	Mercury (0), Venus (0)

◁◁ Saturn and its rings, which are made of ice. Saturn has more than 30 moons. The arrows point to two of them.

Asteroids

As well as the planets, millions of chunks of rock, called asteroids, orbit the Sun. Their path around the Sun is between Mars and Jupiter's. Some of the chunks of rock are smaller than peppercorns. Others are nearly 1000 kilometres across.

Comets

Comets are giant lumps of ice, frozen gas, rock and dust. Most of the time, they travel far from the Sun. When a comet gets close to the Sun, it begins to melt. A long, glowing tail trails out behind it.

Some comets take thousands of years to orbit the Sun, but Halley's Comet can be seen from Earth every 76 years. It last appeared in 1986.

In 1997, Comet Hale-Bopp could be seen in the northern night sky. It will return around the year 4380.

Stars and galaxies

Stars are not star-shaped. Like our Sun, all stars are huge glowing balls of tremendously hot gas.

Giant collections of stars are called galaxies. There are more than 10,000 million galaxies in the Universe. Our Sun is part of a galaxy called the Milky Way.

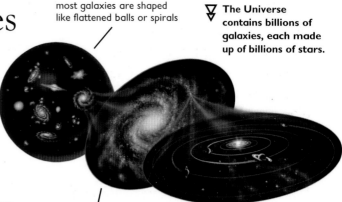

most galaxies are shaped like flattened balls or spirals

▽ **The Universe contains billions of galaxies, each made up of billions of stars.**

the Milky Way is a galaxy of more than 200,000 million stars

our Solar System is part of the Milky Way

The Milky Way

Our galaxy is disc-shaped with spiral arms. The Sun is on one of the arms. On clear nights you can see other parts of the Milky Way in the sky.

Galaxy shapes

Not all galaxies are spirals. Most are shaped like a flattened ball. A few galaxies do not have any particular shape.

◀◀ **Stars are born in clouds of gas and dust called nebulas. This is the Eagle Nebula.**

Burning gas

Stars begin as clumps of hydrogen and helium gas. The gas gets so squashed up that the particles start to join together. They give off huge amounts of energy, just like a hydrogen bomb.

Dying stars

After billions of years, a star runs out of gas to burn. It shrinks and slowly fades away. The biggest stars die differently – in a massive explosion, called a supernova.

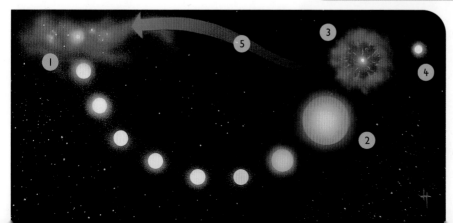

◀◀ **The birth and death of a medium-sized star like the Sun.**

1 nebula (gas cloud where stars are born)
2 red giant (swollen star)
3 planetary nebula (gas cloud around dying star)
4 white dwarf (fading star)
5 gas cloud recycled to make new stars

Space exploration

The Space Age began in October 1957, when the Soviet Union (now Russia) put the satellite *Sputnik 1* into orbit around the Earth.

Since then, human beings have walked on the Moon and and robot spacecraft have visited every planet in our Solar System.

Space race

After the launch of *Sputnik 1*, both the USA and the Soviet Union raced to land people on the Moon. They sent astronauts into orbit around the Earth and unmanned probes to the Moon.

Moon landing

In July 1969, three US astronauts – Michael Collins, Neil Armstrong and Edwin Aldrin – landed on the Moon in the *Apollo 11* spacecraft. Over the next three years there were five more Moon missions.

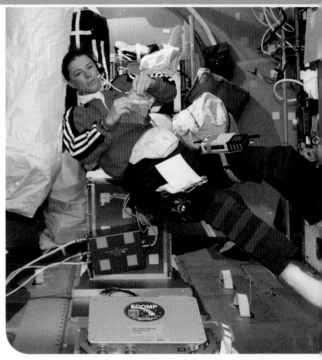

An astronaut inside the Spacelab, a laboratory that is sometimes carried onboard the Space Shuttle.

KEY DATES

1961 Yuri Gagarin is the first man in space
1976 *Viking* sends back pictures of Mars
1989 *Voyager* sends back pictures of Neptune
1990 *Magellan* starts mapping Venus
1995 *Galileo* probe enters Jupiter's orbit
1997 *Sojourner* explores surface of Mars
2000 First crew arrive at International Space Station
2004 *Cassini* sends back pictures of Saturn's rings

The Shuttle uses its rocket fuel tank to blast into space, and its wings to glide back to Earth.

Space Shuttles

Space Shuttle *Columbia* was launched in 1981. It was the first spacecraft that could fly into space many times. Only the main fuel tank is new for each flight.

The Shuttle can carry satellites into orbit or launch space probes.

Space stations

A space station is a place in space where astronauts can live and work. The first space station was *Salyut 1*, launched by the Soviet Union in 1971.

In 1998, the first pieces of a new space station, the ISS (International Space Station), were put together in space. The International Space Station is the biggest-ever space station.

◄◄ The International Space Station contains six laboratories.

An astronaut can ▷▷ move around outside a spacecraft using a jet-powered backpack called an MMU.

Missions to the planets

Since the Moon missions, most space exploration has been carried out by robot space probes. They take photographs and use radar and other instruments to collect information, which they send back to Earth by radio.

Probes have landed on Mars, Venus and Saturn's moon, Titan. They have travelled deep into the atmospheres of Jupiter and Saturn. They have flown past Uranus and Neptune, and they have visited the Sun.

The *Voyager 2* ▷▷ probe took pictures of Jupiter, Saturn, Uranus and Neptune.

DID YOU KNOW?

The first space telescope, Hubble, was launched in 1990. It circles the Earth once every 90 minutes and collects light and other rays from deep space. Chandra X-ray Observatory, put into orbit in 1999, is a telescope that builds up pictures from X-rays.

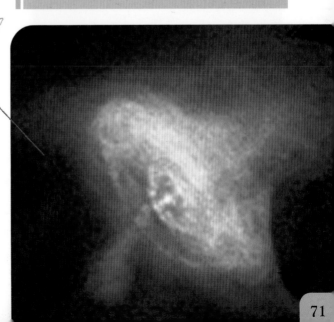

Chandra X-ray Observatory ▷▷ took this picture of the Crab Nebula. It beamed the image to Earth as radio signals.

71

Solids, liquids and gases

Everything around you is either a solid, a liquid or a gas. This is called its state. Whether something is a solid, a liquid or a gas depends on how the particles in it are linked together.

Some materials change from one state to another when they are heated or cooled.

Solids

The particles – the atoms or molecules – that make up solids are close together and do not move around much. Solids can keep their shape without a container.

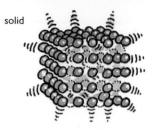
solid

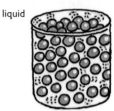
liquid

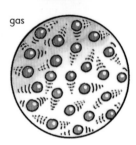
gas

⚠ Atoms in a solid, a liquid and a gas.

▽ Liquid water with solid ice cubes.

Dry ice (frozen carbon dioxide) turning into gas. ⚠

DID YOU KNOW?

When you freeze the gas carbon dioxide, it turns into a solid called dry ice. At room temperature, dry ice turns into a strange, smoky-looking vapour.

Liquids

The particles in liquids are not so close together. Liquids cannot hold their shape and you have to put them in a container to keep them from flowing away.

◁◁ Mercury is a metal, but unlike other metals it is a liquid at room temperature. It is also extremely poisonous.

Three states

At room temperature, water is a liquid. At temperatures below 0 °C, it freezes to become a solid – ice. If you boil water, it starts to turn into a gas – water vapour.

Gases

The particles in gases are not linked to each other at all. They shoot about in all directions. Gases spread out to fill whatever space they are in.

Air

Air is all around you. You cannot see, smell or taste it, but you can feel it moving when the wind blows.

Air is made up of different gases. The main ones are nitrogen and oxygen. Air also contains many other substances, including water vapour, dust, pollen and microscopic creatures.

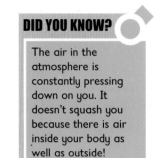

DID YOU KNOW?

The air in the atmosphere is constantly pressing down on you. It doesn't squash you because there is air inside your body as well as outside!

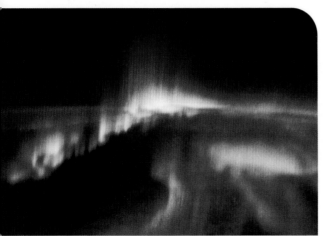

An aurora is an area of coloured lights, high in the atmosphere. This one was photographed from space.

Air to live

Without air, there would be no life on Earth. Plants use the carbon dioxide in the air, together with sunlight and water, to make their food. As they do so, they give off oxygen – the gas that humans and other animals need to breathe.

Earth's atmosphere

Planet Earth is wrapped in layers of air. This blanket of air is called the atmosphere and is several kilometres thick. The atmosphere has different levels. People live in the lowest level, the troposphere. Planes fly in the next layer, the stratosphere.

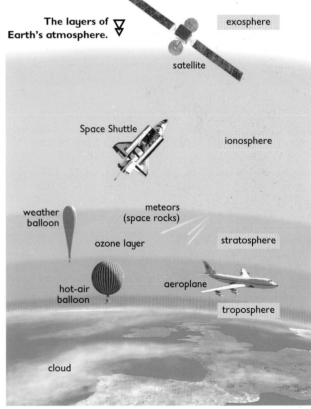

The layers of Earth's atmosphere.

exosphere

satellite

Space Shuttle

ionosphere

weather balloon

meteors (space rocks)

ozone layer

stratosphere

hot-air balloon

aeroplane

troposphere

cloud

Scuba divers carry their own air supply strapped to their back.

Water

Water is the most important liquid on Earth. You could not live without it.

Three-quarters of the planet is covered by water. Most is in oceans, seas and rivers. Some is frozen at the North and South Poles.

△ Rice plants grow in flooded fields called paddies. All plants need water to live.

Water and you

There is more water in you than any other substance. Around 70 per cent of your body is water.

Like all living things, you need water to stay alive. You are losing water all the time – when you breathe, sweat and go to the toilet. You can go for weeks without food, but if you go for three or four days without water, you could die.

DID YOU KNOW?

Water that has fallen as rain eventually forms new rainclouds. This endless cycle is called the water cycle. You can find out more on page 50.

△ Water forms round droplets as it falls to the Earth as rain.

At this village well in ▷▷ India, oxen provide the power to lower and raise the buckets of water.

Water supply

The water from your tap is probably from a river or an artificial lake called a reservoir. The water is cleaned at a water treatment plant before it travels along pipes to your house. Not everyone has water on tap. In some places, people draw water from deep holes in the ground, called wells.

Metals

Gold rings, drinks cans, cars, needles and bridges – all of these things are made from metals. People have been using metals to make things for thousands of years.

Metals may be bright or dull, hard or soft. All of them are good at letting heat and electricity pass through them.

What are metals?

Except for mercury, all metals are solids at room temperature. Most metals are fairly strong. They can be crushed or stretched without breaking. They can also be shaped by hammering or rolling.

△ People have been making things from copper for at least 10,000 years.

◄◄ Inside a blast furnace, crushed iron ore is heated up (smelted) with coke and limestone to produce molten iron.

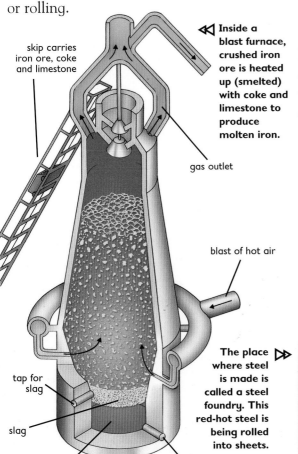

skip carries iron ore, coke and limestone

gas outlet

blast of hot air

tap for slag

slag

molten iron

tap for molten iron

Metal from rock

Most metals are found in rocks called ores. Ores usually contain other substances that have to be removed to get the pure metal. There are different ways to do this.

People make pure iron by smelting – heating up the ore in a furnace. Smelting separates the ore into molten metal and a waste material called slag.

DID YOU KNOW?

Bronze and steel are not pure metals. They are alloys – metals mixed with something else. Bronze is copper mixed with tin. Steel is iron mixed with carbon.

The place where steel is made is called a steel foundry. This red-hot steel is being rolled into sheets. ▷▷

Mining

Mining is getting rocks and minerals out of the ground. Diamonds, coal and metal ores (rocks containing metal) are just some of the materials that people mine.

There are different ways of mining. It depends whether the material is near the surface or way down deep.

At this quarry, workers are mining a very hard rock called granite.

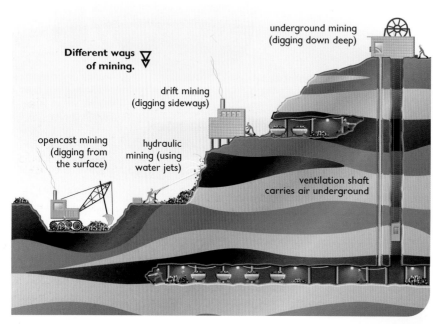

Different ways of mining.

underground mining (digging down deep)

drift mining (digging sideways)

opencast mining (digging from the surface)

hydraulic mining (using water jets)

ventilation shaft carries air underground

Coal

Coal is the remains of plants that lived millions of years ago. The dead plants piled up to form a spongy material called peat. Slowly, other materials settled on top of the peat, squashed it hard and turned it into coal.

Near the surface

Materials that are close to the surface can be mined from quarries or opencast mines. Coal, iron ore and aluminium are sometimes mined like this. Huge power shovels and excavators dig out materials and load them into trucks.

Digging deep

In underground mines miners dig shafts and tunnels to reach ores buried deep below the surface. They remove the ore using explosives or drills.

Mining is a dangerous job. Dusty air can harm miners' lungs, and explosives can cause accidents.

Plastics

Plastic is all around you. It is used to make telephones, computers, toothbrushes, clothes – and countless other things.

Plastics are artificial materials made from chemicals. The basic raw ingredient for most plastics is crude oil.

Some plastic can be recycled to save energy. First it is shredded into tiny pieces.

Making plastic

A plastic is made by linking together small molecules into long chains. Different forms of chain create different types of plastic. Plastics are made in factories, but new ones are invented by chemists in laboratories. The first plastic, Bakelite, appeared in 1909.

blow moulding

compressed air

1. hot plastic put in mould

2. blast of air shapes plastic to mould

3. finished bottle

FAST FACTS ▷▷

Some types of plastic
◎ polythene (plastic bags, drinks bottles)
◎ polystyrene foam (disposable cups)
◎ nylon (carpets, clothes)
◎ polyester (fleece jackets)

extrusion

plastic pellets

△▽ Ways of shaping plastic.

screw

heating element

molten plastic pushed around pipe mould

This roller-blade racer wears plastic from head to toe. It is a tough plastic that will protect him if he falls. ▽

All kinds of plastic

Plastics are amazing. They can be see-through, like glass, or made in any colour. They can be formed into light solid foams, or made into bendy fibres that can be woven into cloth.

Plastic is a good ▷▷ for making toys. It is strong and also easy to clean.

Wood and paper

Wood from tree trunks can be cut and carved to make houses, furniture, boats and other things. It can also be burnt as a fuel to keep you warm.

Wood pulp is used to make paper. Without it, you would have no books to read – and nowhere to write down your homework.

A house built from wood in Montana, USA.

Paper is used for ▷▷ newspapers and many other products.

◁◁ Softwood comes from conifers. Conifers grow faster than broad-leaved trees.

Softwood

There are two types of wood – softwood and hardwood. Softwood comes from conifers, such as pine and spruce. It is useful for building, for making chipboard and for papermaking.

Hardwood

Hardwood comes from broad-leaved trees, such as oak, mahogany and walnut. It is often used to make fine furniture, boats and musical instruments.

Papermaking

At a paper mill, wood is cut into small pieces, called chips, and then soaked in chemicals. This creates wood pulp. Then the pulp is passed through huge machines, which spread it out and drain out the water. Finally it is pressed into long, dry sheets that are stored on rolls.

▽ How paper is made.

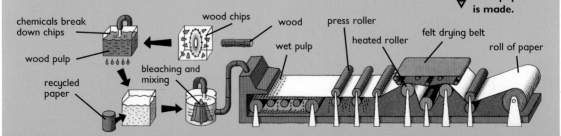

chemicals break down chips
wood pulp
recycled paper
wood chips
wood
wet pulp
bleaching and mixing
press roller
heated roller
felt drying belt
roll of paper

Buildings

Engineers and builders construct all sorts of things – roads, dams, bridges, tunnels and many kinds of buildings.

Builders choose materials to suit the building's size and how it will be used. They also think about the climate in the area and what materials are available there.

DID YOU KNOW?

Very few buildings are taller than 500 m. They include the CN Tower, Canada (553 m), Ostankino Tower, Russia (537 m) and Taipei 101, Taiwan (509 m).

▽ Some of the world's tallest buildings.

7. CN Tower, Canada, 1976: 553

6. Petronas Twin Towers, Malaysia, 1996: 452 m

5. Empire State Building, USA, 1931: 381 m (with mast 449 m)

2. Pharos lighouse, Egypt, about 280 BC: 135 m

4. Eiffel Tower, France, 1889: 300 m

1. Great Pyramid of Khufu, Egypt, about 2580 BC: 147 m

3. Lincoln Cathedral, UK, AD 1307: 160 m

◀◀ In many hot countries bricks are made from clay that is baked hard in the sun.

Traditional materials

In many places, builders still use local materials. In Canada and northern Europe, where there are large forests, many buildings are made of wood. Other traditional materials include stone, clay, mud bricks, bamboo, straw and reeds.

block of flats, Scotland, Europe

mud brick house, Yemen, Middle East

ger (tent), Gobi Desert, central Asia

bamboo hut on stilts, Benin, Africa

△ Some types of house from around the world.

Construction

Many buildings are built around a framework of timber, steel or concrete. Others use solid walls to support the weight of the floors and roof instead.

Building around a ▽ concrete framework.

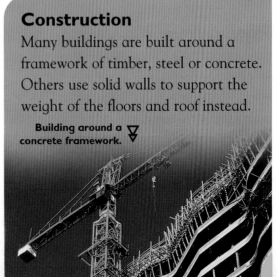

Modern materials

Many modern buildings are built from concrete, steel, bricks and glass. These materials are strong, and they are easy and quick to build with.

Bridges and tunnels

Bridges are structures that allow people or vehicles to cross rivers, valleys, roads or railways. Some span huge distances.

Like bridges, tunnels help people to avoid obstacles. Instead of going over the obstacle, tunnels go under.

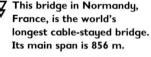

This bridge in Normandy, France, is the world's longest cable-stayed bridge. Its main span is 856 m.

Beam bridges

A tree trunk across a stream is the simplest kind of bridge. The trunk (beam) is supported at each end. A clapper bridge has two or more beams that rest on supports called piers.

Cantilever bridges have sections like clapper bridges, but the sections are supported at their middles instead of at each end.

Using cables

In a suspension bridge, the deck hangs from steel cables, which are strung between the towers. Cable-stayed bridges are similar, but the cables hang directly from the towers.

cantilever bridge

suspension bridge

arch bridge

clapper bridge

cable-stayed bridge

◀◀ Some types of bridge.

Digging deep

Tunnels need supports, usually of steel or concrete, to keep them from collapsing. Deep tunnels are hollowed out using cutting machines, but the very hard rock has to be blown away with explosives.

▽ The Channel Tunnel, which links England and France, has two train tunnels and a service tunnel in between.

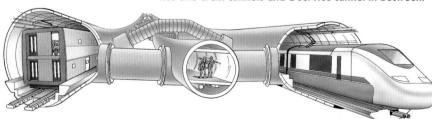

Forces

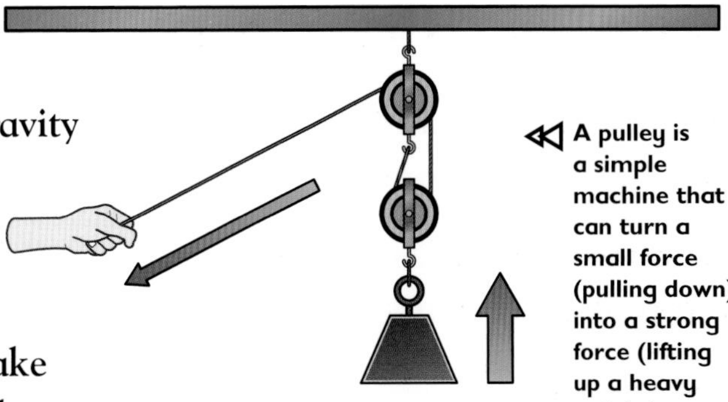

A pulley is a simple machine that can turn a small force (pulling down) into a strong force (lifting up a heavy weight).

Forces are part of everyday life. Gravity is the force that holds you on the Earth. Tension is the force in a stretched rubber band.

A force is a push or pull. It can make an object move, change speed or change direction. When forces act together they can make something stretch, squash, twist, turn or change shape.

Gravity

The force of gravity pulls things together. The bigger the objects, the greater the pull. Because our planet is so massive, there is strong gravity between the Earth and everything that is on or near it.

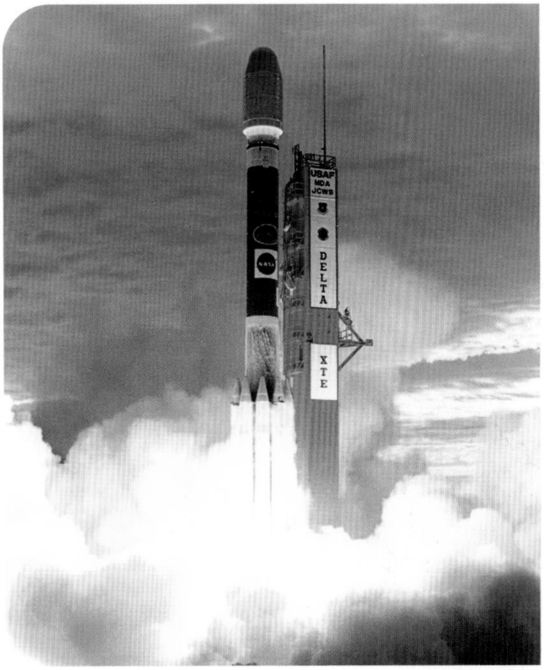

A rocket needs a powerful force – thrust – to escape the pull of Earth's gravity and blast off into space.

Electromagnetic forces

Electricity and magnetism are closely related forces. You can feel the pulling force of a magnet if you hold it close to a piece of iron or steel.

Friction

Friction is a force that tries to stop one material sliding over another. Friction between your shoes and the floor stops you from slipping.

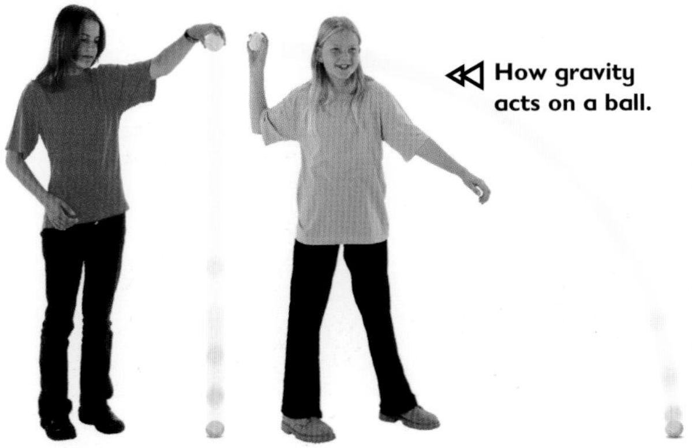

How gravity acts on a ball.

Gravity in action

If you drop one ball and throw another forward from the same height, both balls take the same time to reach the ground. This is because gravity pulls each ball with the same amount of force.

Energy and fuels

Without energy nothing would live, move or change. Your body and everything you do depends on energy.

Energy exists in different forms. Heat, light, electricity and chemical energy are all forms of energy. Nearly all of the energy on Earth comes from the Sun.

Sun gives off heat and light energy.

Green plants use energy from the Sun to grow.

◀◀ How Earth's energy comes from the Sun.

△ Your body uses energy from food so you can be active.

Animals, including humans, get energy from food (plants, or animals that feed on plants).

Fossil fuels (coal, oil and natural gas) formed from the buried remains of plants and animals that lived millions of years ago.

We burn fossil fuels to make electricity and to run our cars.

Changing energy

Energy can change from one form to another. When you kick a ball, your muscles change chemical energy from your food into kinetic energy (movement).

Energy from fuels

We need energy to run our homes, vehicles and factories. Most of this comes from burning fuels such as oil, coal and natural gas. These are called fossil fuels. Once they have been used up, they cannot be replaced.

Oil is found between layers of rock, either underground or beneath the sea floor. An oil rig is a platform used for drilling oil. ▽

△ This car, *Sunraycer*, has solar panels, which collect energy from sunlight and turn it into electricity.

Energy that won't run out

Some fuels, such as wood, are renewable – we can grow more of them. We can also get energy from the Sun, the wind, from moving water and from nuclear power.

Electricity

Electricity is a very useful form of energy. You can turn it on at the flick of a switch, and switch it off again when you don't need it.

Electricity powers trains, lights, televisions and many kinds of machine. It can travel along wires from a power station or battery to wherever it is needed.

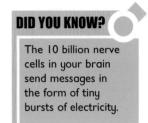

DID YOU KNOW?

The 10 billion nerve cells in your brain send messages in the form of tiny bursts of electricity.

Electricity and atoms

All substances are made from tiny particles called atoms. In the middle of each atom there is a core called the nucleus. Around this nucleus are particles called electrons. Each electron has a tiny electric charge.

Static electricity

When two different materials rub together, electrons move from one material to the other. An electric charge, called static electricity, builds up. Static electricity is what crackles when you pull a woolly jumper over your head.

◁◁ **Rubbing a balloon builds up static electricity – which can make your hair stand on end.**

Current electricity

When electrons flow along a wire, they make current electricity. This is the kind of electricity we get from batteries and mains plugs. In order to flow, the current needs an unbroken path called a circuit. As the current passes through the wires, it can power a light bulb or do other useful jobs.

In this electric circuit, the battery pushes the ▷▷ **electrical current along the wire and through the filament in the light bulb, making it glow.**

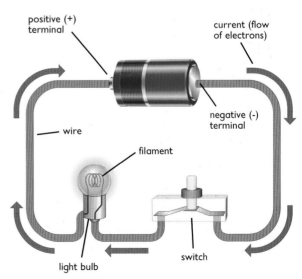

positive (+) terminal

current (flow of electrons)

negative (-) terminal

wire

filament

light bulb

switch

At this power station near St Malo, France, the power of the tides drives the turbines. ◮

Where electricity comes from

Power stations use machines called generators to produce electricity. A generator contains a coil of wire between two spinning magnets. Machines called turbines turn the magnets.

There are different types of power station. Some burn oil, gas or coal to heat water and produce jets of steam that drive the turbines. Others use the power of moving water, the wind or sunlight.

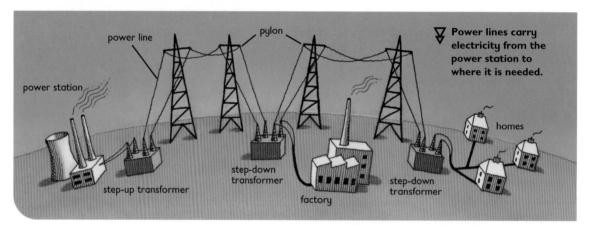

power line   pylon

▽ Power lines carry electricity from the power station to where it is needed.

power station

homes

step-up transformer

step-down transformer

factory

step-down transformer

Transformers

A step-up transformer increases the voltage (pressure) of the electricity as it leaves the power station. This stops energy being lost as it travels along power lines.

Step-down transformers lower the voltage before the electricity goes into homes and workplaces.

Batteries

A battery is a useful way of storing and transporting electricity. Most batteries run out but some can be recharged by connecting them to mains electricity.

Lightning is a flash of electrical ▷▷ charge that shoots through the air.

Lightning

A flash of lightning happens when electrons build up in a storm cloud. Eventually, so much electricity builds up that the electrons leap to another cloud or to the ground. As they flow through the air, the electrons make it glow.

Magnets

Magnetism is a powerful and very useful force. All of the electricity in your house comes from generators that use huge magnets to create electric current.

A magnet can attract other objects or repel (push away) other magnets without touching them.

Pulling power

A magnet is surrounded by an invisible magnetic field. The force is strongest in two places, called the north and south poles.

Magnetic materials

Magnets can only attract things that contain magnetic materials. Iron is the most common. An iron-rich rock called lodestone was one of the first natural magnets that people discovered.

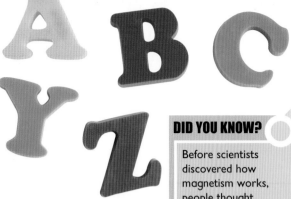

Not all magnets do an important job. Some are just for fun.

DID YOU KNOW?

Before scientists discovered how magnetism works, people thought that magnets had magical power.

Earth has its own magnetic field, with one magnetic pole near the **North Pole**, and the other near the **South Pole**.

North Pole

South Pole

Using magnets

A compass needle is a magnet. It always points north because it lines up with Earth's magnetic field.

Electromagnets are very powerful types of magnet that are used in many electrical machines. They are made by passing an electric current through a coil of wire. When the current is turned off, the magnet loses its power.

◀◀ An electromagnet can be turned on to pick up scrap metal, then turned off to drop it.

Heat and temperature

Heat is a kind of energy. All sorts of things give off heat energy, including your body, cookers, fires and the Sun.

▲ Rays of heat energy from a campfire.

Temperature measures how hot something is. There are different temperature scales. On the Celsius scale, water freezes at 0 °C and boils at 100 °C.

Heat rays

Heat can travel in the form of invisible waves called rays. This is called radiation and it is how heat from the Sun reaches us.

Moving through metal

Metals are good conductors (carriers of heat). Energy from fast-moving atoms in the hot parts of the metal passes to slower-moving atoms in cooler parts. This warms up the cooler parts.

DID YOU KNOW?

If an object is heated, its atoms vibrate (jiggle about) faster. If it cools down, its atoms vibrate more slowly.

Hot air

Heat moves through air in another way. A circulating current forms as hotter material moves away and cooler material takes its place.

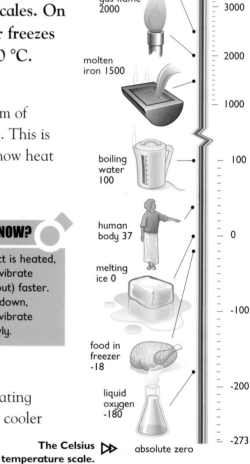

surface of the Sun 6000

temperature in °C

light-bulb filament 2500

gas flame 2000

molten iron 1500

boiling water 100

human body 37

melting ice 0

food in freezer -18

liquid oxygen -180

6000

5000

4000

3000

2000

1000

100

0

-100

-200

-273 absolute zero

The Celsius temperature scale. ▷▷

Hot stars

Stars shine with different colours depending on how hot they are. The hottest stars give off a blue-white light, while cooler stars look reddish.

Hot blue stars in the Butterfly star cluster. ▷▷

Light

Without light, you could not read this book. You can only see things if they give off light, or if they reflect light into your eyes.

Light is a kind of energy. It usually moves in a straight line. Lenses can bend light. Mirrors can bounce back most of the light that falls on them.

When light hits a mirror, it bounces right back. The reflection is reversed, so any writing looks backwards.

A prism splits white light into all the colours of the spectrum.

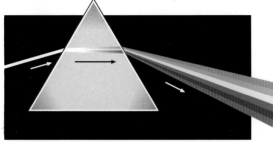

A laser beam can mend the eye to correct poor sight.

Colours

White light contains all the colours of the rainbow. This is called the spectrum.

A prism is a see-through block, often pyramid-shaped, that allows you to see the colours in white light. It bends the different colours by different amounts.

DID YOU KNOW?

Nothing can travel faster than the speed of light. Light travels at around 300,000 km per second.

The light bulb was invented in the 1870s. Before then, people burned candles or gas or oil lamps to get light.

Using light

Light bulbs and torches allow us to see when it is dark. Solar power plants use light energy from the Sun to produce electricity.

Tiny pulses of laser light carry telephone calls, TV pictures and computer data around the world. And laser light is even used to carry out eye surgery.

Sounds

You cannot see sound waves, but you can hear them through your ears. Sounds allow us to talk to each other and to listen to music.

Sounds include the squeak of a mouse and the blast of a foghorn. Some sounds, such as dog whistles, are outside our range of hearing.

Frequency

Sounds can be high or low. It depends on the sound's frequency – how fast the sound wave vibrates (wobbles). The higher a sound's frequency, the higher-pitched the sound.

Range of hearing

Frequency is measured in hertz (Hz), or vibrations per second. Most people can hear sounds between about 20 Hz and 20,000 Hz. Sounds above the range of our hearing are called ultrasonic sounds.

Sounds on the move

Sound waves can travel through solids, liquids and gases but not through space. They travel through air at a speed of around 330 metres per second. When sound waves hit hard surfaces, they bounce back as echoes.

◀◀ Hitting a drum produces sound waves that travel through the air.

Concorde ▶▶ was the first passenger plane to fly faster than the speed of sound.

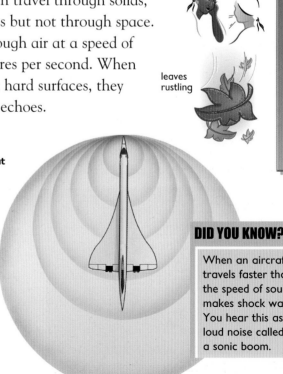

Noise levels are measured in decibels (dB). ▽ ▽

noise level in decibels

- space shuttle lift-off — 180
- very loud personal stereo — 160
- damage to ears — 140
- road drill — 120
- rock concert — 100
- some discomfort to ears
- telephone ringing — 80
- normal conversation — 60
- — 40
- leaves rustling — 20
- — 0

DID YOU KNOW?

When an aircraft travels faster than the speed of sound, it makes shock waves. You hear this as a loud noise called a sonic boom.

Ships and boats

For thousands of years, ships and boats have carried people and cargoes. Today most people travel long distances by air, but ships still carry cargo.

Submarines travel under the sea. They are used to carry missiles or to explore the ocean depths.

This three-person submarine, *Nautile*, is fitted with cameras, floodlights and two remote-controlled robotic arms.

Engines and sails

Most modern ships have engines that power underwater propellers. Some boats have engines, but they may also be driven by oars, paddles or sails.

Sails use the force of the wind to push the boat along. Yachts are sailing boats used for racing or leisure.

Modern cargo ships

Tankers and bulk carriers carry a cargo such as oil or grain, which is pumped on board through a pipe.

Container ships carry hundreds of truck-sized metal boxes called containers. Each container may hold something different, such as books, toasters or jeans.

At a busy port like this one in Italy, huge cranes load containers on to container ships, trains or lorries.

Fighting ships

A navy is a force that fights at sea. It has small ships called destroyers and frigates that carry guided missiles. Some navies have huge aircraft carriers than can transport as many as 90 aircraft.

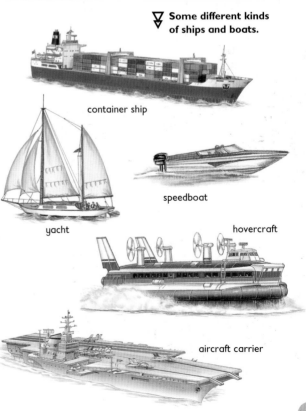

Some different kinds of ships and boats.

container ship

yacht

speedboat

hovercraft

aircraft carrier

Trains

Trains are the fastest way of getting around on land. High-speed passenger trains travel at up to 300 kilometres per hour.

Freight trains are slower, but they can carry thousands of tonnes of goods such as oil, chemicals and cars.

This freight train in the USA is carrying coal.

'The Rocket' was one of the first steam locomotives. It entered service on the Liverpool and Manchester Railway in 1830.

This test train, called a maglev, uses magnets to make the train float above the track. It can reach speeds of 400 km/h.

Engine power

A train is made up of a locomotive and carriages. The locomotive pulls the train along. The first locomotives ran on steam, but today's are powered by diesel fuel, electricity or a mix of the two.

Along the tracks

Railway track is made of steel rails laid on concrete or wooden blocks called sleepers. Viaducts (high bridges) carry the railway across valleys. Tunnels carry it through hills.

Signals

Railway track is divided into sections, with a signal at the start of each section. A train can pass a signal only if it shows 'go'. Many trains have a computer that automatically stops them if the signal shows 'stop'. This helps to prevent crashes.

Underground trains

In some cities underground railways transport people below street level. The first, the London Underground, opened in 1863. The underground with the most stations (468) is the New York City Subway.

A metro (underground) station in Paris, France.

Cars

There are around 500 million cars in the world. They include small city cars, four-wheel drives that can go cross-country and super-fast racing cars.

There are different kinds of motor racing. Formula 1 takes place on purpose-built tracks or closed city roads.

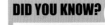

DID YOU KNOW?

The world's fastest car is *Thrust SSC*. Its record speed is 1228 km/h and it is powered by two jet engines.

Powering cars

Almost all car engines burn petrol or diesel fuel, but this produces exhaust fumes. Hybrid cars make less fumes because they use battery power at low speeds.

Car safety

Cars have safety glass, seat belts and air bags to help protect passengers if there is an accident. Even so, car accidents kill over a million people worldwide each year.

◁◁ **Most cars are made by robots like this robotic arm.**

The parts of a car

A car engine produces power to drive the wheels. The transmission takes power to the wheels, through the gearbox. Gears allow the car to work well at different speeds.

The driver uses the steering wheel to change direction, the accelerator to speed up and the brakes to slow down or stop.

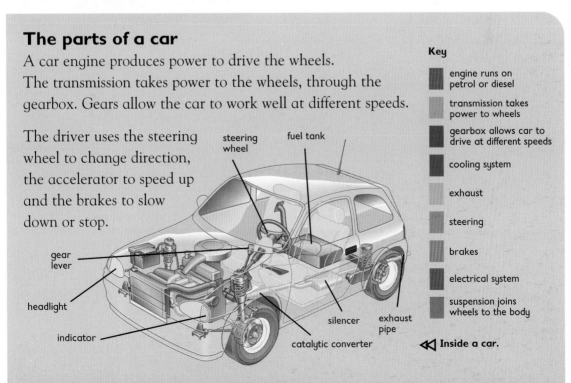

steering wheel

fuel tank

gear lever

headlight

indicator

silencer

exhaust pipe

catalytic converter

Key

engine runs on petrol or diesel

transmission takes power to wheels

gearbox allows car to drive at different speeds

cooling system

exhaust

steering

brakes

electrical system

suspension joins wheels to the body

◁◁ **Inside a car.**

Aircraft

You couldn't fly off on holiday before there were aircraft! Aeroplanes, helicopters, balloons and airships are all types of aircraft. Some of these flying machines need wings and engines. Others are light enough to float through the air.

The first aeroplane was built in 1903 and made of wood. Aeroplanes today are made of light, very strong materials.

▽ A Boeing 747 airliner can carry over 300 passengers.

MIG-29 fighter plane

Aeroplanes and helicopters

All aeroplanes have wings and an engine. The shape of the wings is important. Straight wings work best for carrying heavy loads, but arrow-shaped wings are better for fast flying. A helicopter has long, thin wings called blades that spin around to lift it into the air.

Bell 222 police and rescue helicopter

Schweizer stunt glider

At a busy airport, planes take off and land all the time. People in the control tower help this happen safely. ▽

control tower

runway

terminal

docking bay

raillink

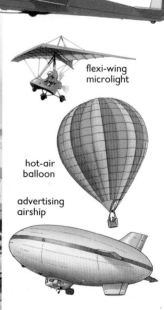

flexi-wing microlight

hot-air balloon

advertising airship

△ Some different kinds of aircraft

The aeroplane's engine moves it through the air. Tiny microlights use a motorcycle engine, but most bigger aircraft have powerful jet engines. Jet airliners fly along at over 850 kilometres per hour. Fighter jets fly even faster – at more than twice the speed of sound.

KEY DATES

1783 First hot-air balloon flight in France

1852 Henri Giffard makes the first airship flight

1903 The first aeroplane flight, by the Wright brothers' *Flyer*

1937 Frank Whittle designs the first jet engine

1976 Concorde is the first supersonic airliner

1999 First round-the-world balloon flight

Jet engines

Jet engines are amazingly powerful. In a jet engine, air is sucked in at the front, compressed and forced into a combustion chamber. Fuel is added, and the fuel and air burn. This produces very hot gases, which shoot out of the back, driving the aircraft forward. Some jet engines, called turbofans, have a huge fan at the front to help collect the air.

This is what a turbofan jet engine looks like inside.

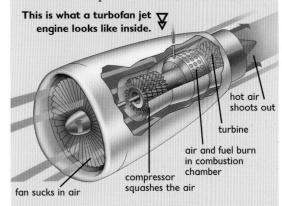

hot air shoots out

turbine

air and fuel burn in combustion chamber

compressor squashes the air

fan sucks in air

Gliders

Gliders look like one-person aeroplanes but they do not have engines. They are very light and they use the force of the wind to stay up. A glider can go higher using thermals, currents of warm air that rise from the ground on a sunny day.

Balloons and airships

Airships have engines and can travel in any direction. Balloons travel where the wind blows them.

To float, a balloon or airship has to be lighter than the air around. Airships and gas balloons are usually filled with helium gas, which is very light. Hot-air balloons have burners that heat the air inside them. Hot air is lighter than cool air, so the balloon rises.

Hot-air balloons are used for fun or racing. Gas balloons are used for weather forecasting and scientific experiments. Airships are sometimes used for taking photographs from the air.

DID YOU KNOW?

The first air passengers were a sheep, a duck and a cockerel! In 1783 they travelled in a hot-air balloon built by Joseph and Etienne Montgolfier. Later that year, a Montgolfier balloon carried two men across Paris.

Bicycles

After walking, bicycles are the world's most common form of transport. They are cheap to buy, cost nothing to run and they do not produce pollution.

There are many different kinds of bicycles. Mountain bikes are good over rough ground; touring bikes are comfortable over long journeys.

This bicycle is being used to transport bananas in India.

Motorcycles

A motorcycle is a bicycle with an engine. It has a steel frame, like a bicycle, and the engine, fuel tank, saddle and other parts are bolted to this. The first motorcycle with a petrol engine was made in 1885 by the German Gottleib Daimler.

A motorcycle.

Bicycle history

The first bicycles were wooden, with iron tyres and no brakes or pedals. The first pedal bicycle was built in 1839, and in 1888 air-filled tyres were invented. Lightweight bicycles, BMX bikes and mountain bikes were introduced in the 1970s.

Powering a bicycle

Bicycles run on muscle power. Pressing on the pedals turns the chain wheel, which pulls on the chain. The chain turns the back wheel, and drives the bike along. Many bicycles have gears to make riding easier.

The parts of a racing bike.

Key

1	saddle
2	frame
3	handlebars
4	gear levers
5	brake levers
6	tyre
7	wheel
8	pedal
9	chain wheel
10	chain gears
11	brakes

Weapons

The earliest weapons were sharp stones, pointed sticks, slings, and bows and arrows. Prehistoric people used them to kill wild animals – and to attack other people.

Since then, all sorts of weapons have been invented, from simple swords to the nuclear bomb.

DID YOU KNOW?

Materials used for body armour have included leather, metal and bullet-proof Kevlar. Armour plating also protects vehicles, such as tanks.

Cutting edge

The first swords were made over 5000 years ago. The Roman *gladius* was a short, stabbing sword. Medieval warriors had huge, two-handed broadswords.

Firearms

Early cannons fired metal or stone balls, but often blew up in the firer's face. Handguns were difficult to use, too, because gunpowder would not fire in wet weather. Then shells were invented – metal cases to hold the bullet.

Until machine guns, pulling the trigger of a gun fired only one bullet.

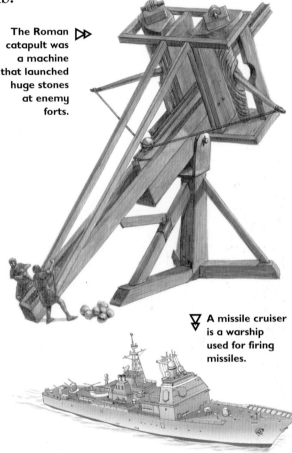

The Roman ▷▷ catapult was a machine that launched huge stones at enemy forts.

▽▽ A missile cruiser is a warship used for firing missiles.

▽ A stealth bomber is designed so that radar finds it hard to detect.

Modern weapons

Bombs are dropped from aircraft or fired from missile launchers. Today's smart bombs and laser-guided weapons use the latest technology to land on target.

Other modern weapons include hidden mines which explode on touch, poison gas and even deadly germs.

Television

Television broadcasts news stories, sporting events, dramas, game shows, cartoons and commercials. Some programmes help you learn and some are just for fun.

Almost every home in the developed world has at least one television set. In poorer nations the number of homes with televisions is growing fast.

▽ Inside a television recording studio.

Pictures into signals

Like an ordinary camera, a television camera collects light from a moving scene. Inside the camera a light-sensitive device turns the pattern of light into electrical signals. Sound is added to the signals later.

△ The first person to show how television could work was the Scottish engineer John Logie Baird in 1926.

Signals into your home

Television signals are sent to your television set by radio waves, via satellites or through underground cables. Your TV receives signals from many different television stations. It has a tuner to pick out the signal from the station you want.

Signals into pictures

Your television breaks down the signal into separate signals for red, green and blue, and for sound. It uses these signals to recreate the picture on the screen and to make sound.

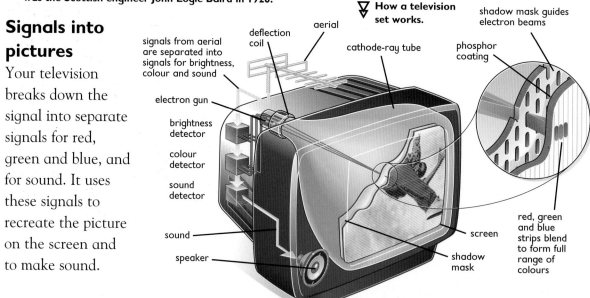

▽ How a television set works.

signals from aerial are separated into signals for brightness, colour and sound

deflection coil

aerial

cathode-ray tube

shadow mask guides electron beams

phosphor coating

electron gun

brightness detector

colour detector

sound detector

sound

speaker

screen

shadow mask

red, green and blue strips blend to form full range of colours

Cameras

Cameras are devices that take photographs. Photographs can be simple holiday snaps, as well as pictures in newspapers, books or art exhibitions.

Some photos do an important job, such as recording a crime scene or helping to advertise a new product.

△ **Julia Margaret Cameron (1815–1879) took this photographic portrait of Alice Liddell (for whom *Alice in Wonderland* was written).**

Types of camera

There are two main kinds of camera – film cameras and digital cameras. Film cameras record the image on to film that has light-sensitive chemicals. Digital cameras store the image on a microchip.

▽ **To take an action photo, the camera's shutter must open and close very quickly.**

Capturing the image

When you take a photograph, the camera's shutter opens to let light in. The lens collects the light and focuses it to make the image. Most cameras focus automatically.

▽ **The parts of an SLR (single-lens reflex) camera.**

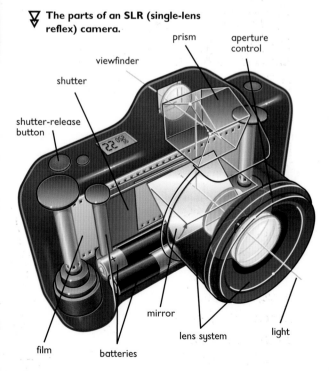

prism

aperture control

viewfinder

shutter

shutter-release button

film

batteries

mirror

lens system

light

Prints

A film image is called a negative. Areas that were light on the original are dark on the film, while dark images appear light. To create a positive print, you shine light through the negative on to a piece of light-sensitive paper.

Digital cameras store the image as binary code (a list of 1s and 0s). This can be read by a computer to display or print the image.

Communications

Speaking, writing and signalling with your hands are all kinds of communication. So are talking on the telephone, sending texts or watching television.

Modern machines let you swap information more quickly than ever before. In the past, people relied on horseback messengers or even smoke signals.

Written word

Writing first appeared in Mesopotamia (now Iraq) about 5000 years ago. Writing allows us to share information through newspapers, books, emails – or even recipes.

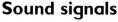 Optical cable carries voice signals as pulses of light. One cable can carry 40,000 phone calls at once.

KEY DATES

1450	Invention of the printing press
1837	Telegraph sends signals along wires
1876	Invention of the telephone
1895	Marconi sends a message using radio waves
1962	First communication by satellite
1969	ARPANET (early Internet) goes live

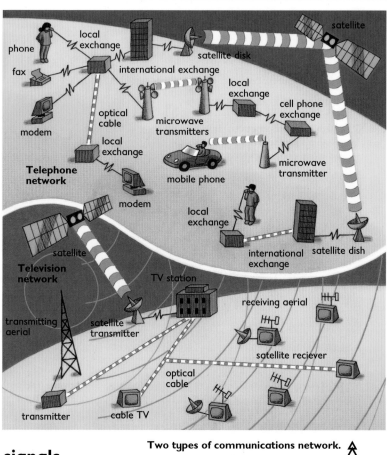

Two types of communications network.

Sound signals

Telephones allow you to speak to other people long-distance. They change the sounds into signals. These might be patterns of electric current that travel along wires, or pulses of light that travel along optical fibres (bundles of thin glass strands).

Mobile phones send their signals as microwaves, a kind of radio wave. Radio waves are also used to broadcast radio and television signals.

Computers

People run businesses, do homework and play games on computers. They also use them to explore the Internet or to look at photos from digital cameras.

Computers are part of everyday life, but they have not been around very long. Until around 1980, only scientists and engineers used computers.

△ Even very young children use computer toys.

Hardware and software

Computers are made up of hardware and software. The hardware means the objects you can touch, such as the computer screen, CD drive and keyboard. The software means the programs that your computer uses to do different jobs.

The different parts of a ▽ personal computer (PC).

scanner · loudspeaker · monitor · external storage unit · printer · joystick · central processor · CD-ROM drive · keyboard · floppy-disk drive · mouse

Computers at work

Factories have computer-controlled machines and robots. Businesses use computers to write letters, handle information and keep accounts. Designers use computers to create all sorts of things, from posters and magazines to toasters and mobile phones.

This pilot is training in a flight simulator – a ▽ cockpit on the ground which uses computers to create the feeling of flying a real aircraft.

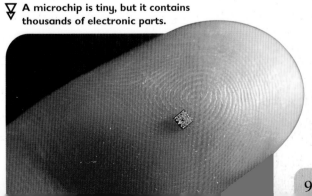

Computer chips

At the heart of every computer is a tiny microchip, or microprocessor. It is a small slice of silicon that has an extremely complicated electronic circuit on it. The microchip processes information sent to it by a program.

Computers also have memory chips, to store information.

▽ A microchip is tiny, but it contains thousands of electronic parts.

Internet

The Internet is a huge computer network that makes it easy for people around the world to share information. It links together many small networks of computers.

You can use the Internet to send and receive electronic mail (email) and to visit web sites.

Getting connected

To use the Internet you need a computer and a link to the network, such as a modem and telephone line or a broadband connection. If you do not have a computer, you can use one at your local library or Internet café.

▽ Schoolchildren using the Internet.

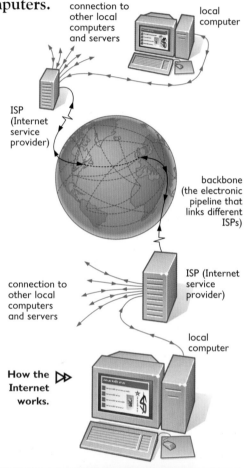

connection to other local computers and servers

local computer

ISP (Internet service provider)

backbone (the electronic pipeline that links different ISPs)

connection to other local computers and servers

ISP (Internet service provider)

local computer

How the ▷▷ Internet works.

Web sites

The worldwide web is part of the Internet. It is made up of thousands of independent computers, called web servers. They store information in files called web sites.

Web sites may contain video clips, animations, music and pictures. Some web sites are shops that sell products such as music.

History of the Internet

The idea of networking computers began in the 1950s. It developed as a way for US army units to communicate. During the 1970s universities began to form networks to swap research. In 1990, the worldwide web was developed, with web sites that were free for anyone to access.

Numbers

We use numbers in almost everything we do. We count the number of children in a class, look for a house number in a street or use page numbers in a book.

Early people probably recorded numbers with stone counters, or by making marks on a stick or piece of clay. In time, people used symbols for numbers instead.

Hindu-Arabic numbers

We use the Hindu-Arabic system for writing and counting numbers. It was first used in the 6th century in India and has just ten number symbols – 0, 1, 2, 3, 4, 5, 6, 7, 8 and 9.

Prime numbers

Prime numbers are numbers that cannot be made by multiplying smaller numbers together. In this table, they are in the red squares. The numbers in the white squares can all be made by multiplying smaller numbers together.

▽ Prime numbers are in the red squares and composite numbers are in the white squares.

1	2	3	4	5	6	7	8	9	10
11	12	13	14	15	16	17	18	19	20
21	22	23	24	25	26	27	28	29	30
31	32	33	34	35	36	37	38	39	40
41	42	43	44	45	46	47	48	49	50
51	52	53	54	55	56	57	58	59	60
61	62	63	64	65	66	67	68	69	70
71	72	73	74	75	76	77	78	79	80
81	82	83	84	85	86	87	88	89	90
91	92	93	94	95	96	97	98	99	100

symbols (numerals)		
Arabic	**Hindu**	**Roman**
1	९	I
2	२	II
3	३	III
4	४	IV
5	५	V
6	६	VI
7	७	VII
8	८	VIII
9	९	IX
10	९०	X
15	९५	XV
50	५०	L
100	९००	C
500	५००	D
1000	९०००	M

⚠ Different number systems.

We tell the time using a 12-hour or a 24-hour clock. This clock face has Roman numerals. ⚠

Changing meanings

We can use the Hindu-Arabic system to write any number. The position of each number symbol affects its meaning. In the number 765, for example, the 5 stands for five units, the 6 for six tens and the 7 for seven hundreds.

Shapes

Every object has a shape. Some shapes, such as a kitten or a rock, are irregular.

Some shapes, such as triangles, squares, cubes and spheres, are regular. They follow special mathematical rules.

Plane shapes

Two-dimensional shapes, or plane shapes, have length and width but no thickness. Triangles, squares, circles and ellipses (ovals) are all plane shapes.

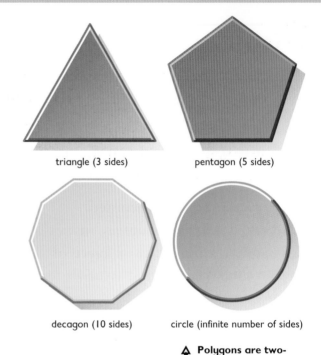

triangle (3 sides)

pentagon (5 sides)

decagon (10 sides)

circle (infinite number of sides)

Polygons are two-dimensional shapes with straight sides.

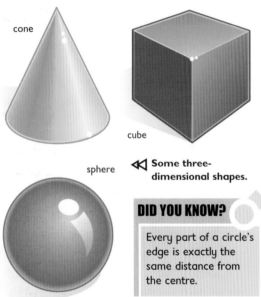

cone

cube

sphere

◀◀ Some three-dimensional shapes.

DID YOU KNOW?

Every part of a circle's edge is exactly the same distance from the centre.

Solid shapes

Three-dimensional shapes, or solid shapes, have length, width and height. Cubes, cones and spheres are examples of solid shapes.

Which shape?

A plane shape with straight sides is called a polygon. A solid shape with straight sides is called a polyhedron. The flat parts of a polyhedron are called its faces. A cube is a regular polyhedron with six identical square faces.

Angles

Angles are measured in degrees (°). A complete turn of a circle is 360°. A quarter-turn is 90° (a right angle). A half-turn is 180°.

Measuring ▷▷ angles in degrees.

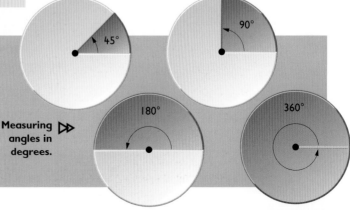

45°

90°

180°

360°

Graphs

A graph is a way of showing data as a picture instead of a long string of numbers. Graphs make it easy to compare sets of numbers and they also show up any patterns.

A graph might show the information as a curved line, a set of coloured bars or as slices of a pie.

DID YOU KNOW?

Computer software can turn data into graphs for you.

Line graphs

Line graphs are useful for showing how things change over time. They can be used to plot the changing temperature of a sick patient, or to show how a child gets taller as she grows older.

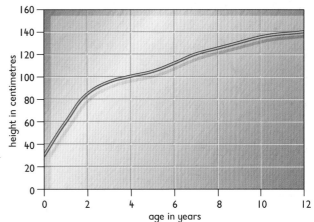

A line graph showing how a girl ▷▷ grows taller as she gets older.

A bar chart to show how a group ▽ of children travel to school.

Bar charts

Bar charts are useful for comparing different numbers, such as the temperatures at different holiday resorts in the same month, or how many vehicles of different types drive past your school in a day. The taller a bar, the bigger the number it stands for.

Pie charts

A pie chart looks like a pie cut into slices. It can be used to show what part of the whole group splits into smaller categories – for example, it can be used to show the favourite colours in a group of children or what pets they own.

A pie chart to show the favourite ▷▷ colours among a group of children.

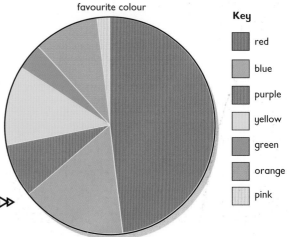

favourite colour

Key

- red
- blue
- purple
- yellow
- green
- orange
- pink

103

Stories and poems

All around the world people tell stories. Some stories help to make sense of the things that happen in the world. Others just entertain.

People were telling stories long before writing existed. Today people read stories in books and magazines, watch stories on television and listen to them on the radio.

Myths

The oldest stories are myths – stories that help to explain the Universe. They form part of the culture of a people, or even part of their religious beliefs. The Asante people of West Africa tell many myths about the trickster-god Anansi.

△ The Asante god Anansi as a spider, about to trick a bird into giving him some bananas.

Legends

Legends are stories that are probably based on real events, but have become exaggerated over time. The legend of the Pied Piper tells of a man who got rid of a town's rats by playing his pipe. When the people did not pay up, the Pied Piper played again – and all the children followed him out of town.

How the world began

Different cultures have their own myths to explain how the world was made. The ancient Japanese said that the twin gods Isanagi and Isanami created the world by stirring a sea of mud with a spear.

Isanami (left) and ▷▷ Isanagi (right) creating islands out of the ocean.

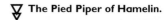
▽ The Pied Piper of Hamelin.

Folk and fairy tales

Folk and fairy tales are made-up stories about extraordinary or magical adventures. The *Arabian Nights*, which was first written down around 1000 years ago, drew on tales from India, Persia, Greece, Egypt and China. It includes the stories of Aladdin and Sinbad the Sailor.

A genie appearing to Aladdin, one of the heroes in the *Arabian Nights*.

Early literature

Literature means great stories that have been written down. The earliest writings were epics – long poems that told of gods, heroes and monsters. They include the Indian *Mahabharata* and the ancient Greek poems, *The Iliad* and *The Odyssey*.

Poems and novels

Writers can tell their story in different forms. In a poem, the words follow a rhythm. There may be a set number of beats in each line. Sometimes, the lines rhyme.

A novel tells a story in ordinary language (prose). Novels include crime stories, romances and comedies. Some have exciting plots. Others try to describe how people think.

'The Tiger', a poem by the English artist and poet William Blake.

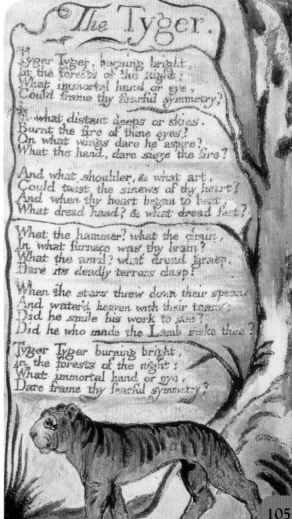

Stories for children

Some authors write specially for children. They include Hergé (1907–1983), who wrote and illustrated *The Adventures of Tintin*, and JK Rowling, author of the Harry Potter books. Charles Dickens (1812–1870) did not aim his books at children, but they are enjoyed by adults and children alike.

A scene from *David Copperfield* by Charles Dickens.

Plays and the theatre

Have you ever been in a play? A play is a story that is acted out. All over the world, people enjoy watching and acting in plays.

Many people go to the theatre to see plays being performed live. Plays can make you laugh, cry – or even give you a fright.

Western drama

The ancient Greeks put on powerful plays called tragedies that had unhappy endings. They also wrote comedies – plays that end happily and make people laugh.

From the 1500s, people began to go to theatres to see professional actors. William Shakespeare lived at this time. Today, people can watch plays at home on television.

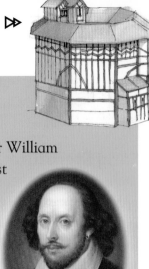

Shakespeare's actors performed at the Globe Theatre, London. ▷▷

William Shakespeare

The English writer William Shakespeare's most famous tragedies are *Hamlet*, *Macbeth*, *Othello* and *King Lear*. He also wrote comedies, such as *A Midsummer Night's Dream* and *Twelfth Night*.

William Shakespeare (1564–1616) △

▽ The most common type of theatre has an arch that frames the stage.

Eastern drama

Japanese No plays use music, dancing, costumes and masks. Beijing opera is a Chinese theatre form. It features acrobatics, opera singing and dance.

This demon mask ▷▷ comes from Japanese No theatre.

Key

1	arch	6	scenery and props
2	lights	7	dressing room
3	curtain	8	wardrobe (costume) room
4	fireproof safety curtain	9	lighting control room
5	trapdoor	10	spare scenery and props

Dance

When you dance, you move your body – usually in time to music. You might dance to celebrate, to entertain or just to have fun!

Ballet and Indian dance are two kinds of performance dancing. Dances for fun include salsa and breakdancing.

Indian dancers use 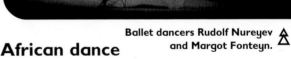 their bodies to tell stories about Hindu gods and heroes.

Indian dance

Indian dances were first performed in Hindu temples over 2000 years ago. The dancers often wear bells on their ankles. Their moves, gestures and expressions are very graceful.

FAST FACTS

Ballet
◉ Ballet began in France.
◉ Two of the most famous ballet dancers were Rudolf Nureyev and Margot Fonteyn.
◉ A ballet dance for two people is called a pas de deux.

This dance  exercise helps dancers to keep their bodies supple.

Ballet dancers Rudolf Nureyev and Margot Fonteyn.

African dance

In Africa, people dance to celebrate weddings, harvests and other happy times. Dancers often sway their hips and stamp out the beat with their feet.

Folk dance

Every place has its own folk dances. In Britain, morris dancing is the best-known type. South-east Asian folk dancers dress up as dragons or lions to frighten away evil spirits.

These women are dancing in Angola, south-western Africa.

Music

Music is very powerful. It can make you dance or it can make you cry. It can calm you down or cheer you up.

Music is as old as human beings. Prehistoric people chanted and made simple music by clapping their hands or banging two sticks together.

A carving of ancient Assyrian musicians from the 7th century BC. ▽▽

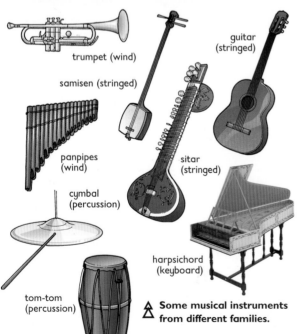

trumpet (wind)

guitar (stringed)

samisen (stringed)

panpipes (wind)

sitar (stringed)

cymbal (percussion)

harpsichord (keyboard)

tom-tom (percussion)

△△ Some musical instruments from different families.

Writing music

In most parts of the world, music is never written down. It is learned and passed on as it is played. Western music is written down on a set of lines called a stave. Each note is named after a letter from A to G.

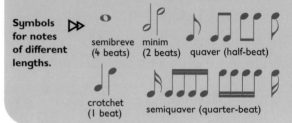

Symbols for notes of different lengths.

semibreve (4 beats)　minim (2 beats)　quaver (half-beat)

crotchet (1 beat)　semiquaver (quarter-beat)

Musical ingredients

All music is made up of notes, which can be high or low. Notes can be played together (in harmony) or one after the other (in a melody). Longer and shorter notes are put together in a pattern called a rhythm. Almost all music is a mix of harmony, melody and rhythm.

Types of instrument

There are thousands of different musical instruments around the world, but they all belong to just a few families.

Stringed instruments, such as violins, guitars and sitars, have strings that you pluck or press.

Wind instruments, such as flutes and panpipes, make a sound when you blow into them. They are often made of wood or metal.

Keyboard instruments, such as pianos, have keys that you press in order to hit a string inside and make it vibrate (wobble).

You play percussion instruments by banging, shaking or even scraping them. They include drums, maracas and xylophones.

Types of music

Music comes in many styles. It can be played or sung to honour gods or just to entertain. Folk music is the music that is played by ordinary people. Classical music is more serious and complex.

Quechua Indians in Peru playing folk music.

◀◀ The composer Wolfgang Amadeus Mozart as a child, performing with his father and sister.

Western classical music

Classical music in Europe is performed by orchestras or smaller groups, either on its own or to accompany an opera or ballet. Bach, Mozart and Beethoven are three of the best-known classical composers.

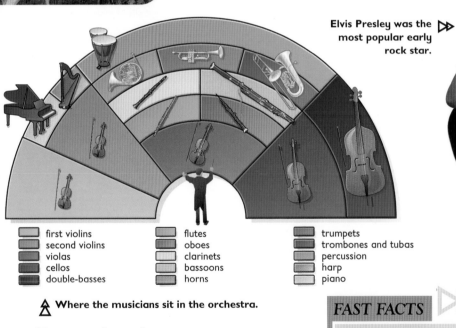

Elvis Presley was the ▶▶ most popular early rock star.

first violins
second violins
violas
cellos
double-basses

flutes
oboes
clarinets
bassoons
horns

trumpets
trombones and tubas
percussion
harp
piano

⊿ Where the musicians sit in the orchestra.

Pop and rock

Pop music began in the USA in the 1950s, when American teenagers began to listen to a new kind of music called rock 'n' roll.

Today, pop music is made up of lots of different styles. Disco, rap, hip-hop, soul and heavy metal are just a few.

FAST FACTS

Best-Selling Singles
"Candle in the Wind 1997" – Elton John
"White Christmas" – Bing Crosby
"Rock Around the Clock" – Bill Haley and the Comets
"I Want to Hold Your Hand" – The Beatles
"Hey Jude" – The Beatles
"It's Now or Never" – Elvis Presley
"I Will Always Love You" – Whitney Houston
"Hound Dog" – Elvis Presley
"Diana" – Paul Anka
"I'm a Believer" – The Monkees

Films and cartoons

Films, or movies, are moving pictures that tell a story. They are one of the most popular kinds of entertainment. Today most films are watched at home on television rather than at the cinema.

Not all films contain human actors. Animations are films that star cartoon characters instead.

Early movies

The first films were short, but soon longer films, called features, were produced. They did not have sound but were sometimes accompanied by live music. *The Jazz Singer* (1927) was the first big film that had sound.

Charlie Chaplin (1889–1977) was a popular silent movie star.

Classic films

During the 1930s and 1940s, Hollywood produced some wonderful films that are still enjoyed today. They include *Gone With the Wind* (1939), *The Wizard of Oz* (1939), *Citizen Kane* (1941) and *Casablanca* (1942). *The Wizard of Oz* was one of the first films to use colour.

How a film is made.

Now in 70 mm. wide screen and full stereophonic sound!

DAVID O. SELZNICK'S PRODUCTION OF MARGARET MITCHELL'S "GONE WITH THE WIND"

A poster for the film *Gone With the Wind* (1939).

Key

1. director
2. actors
3. camera crew
4. cinematographer is the director of photography
5. sound team
6. lighting team
7. continuity assistant checks details of the scene
8. make-up artist
9. editor
10. sound mixer

Special effects

Since the 1970s, film-makers have used more and more special effects. Some effects are created using models. Most are produced on computer.

Animated films

Toy Story (1995) was the first animated feature film made entirely on computer. Animated films are made from a series of pictures similar to the frames of a cartoon strip. The pictures may be drawings, including computer drawings, or they may be photographs of models.

British animator Nick Park, who created the characters Wallace and Gromit, uses clay models for his films.

Still cartoons

A cartoon can also be a single picture or a comic strip. Cartoons that are just one picture appear in newspapers and magazines. They often make a joke about the news of the day.

Comic strips

Comic strips also appear in newspapers and magazines. They use a few pictures (frames) to tell a funny story. 'Peanuts' first appeared in 1950. It features a boy called Charlie Brown and his dog, Snoopy.

A 'Peanuts' comic strip by Charles Schulz.

Comics

Comics are magazines that are full of comic-strip stories. Comics posted on the Internet are called webcomics.

Some comics are about superheroes, such as Superman or Spiderman. Japanese comics (manga) are popular around the world. Astroboy, who first appeared in 1952, was an early manga character.

Design

This book has been designed using a computer. The designer chose the typefaces and pictures and put them all together.

Design is the process of deciding how something should be made and how it should look.

What is designed?

Books and advertisements are designed by graphic designers. Industrial designers work on new products, such as kettles, cars or food and drink. Fashion designers create new clothes. Landscape designers plan gardens, parks or whole towns.

The glass Coca-Cola bottle was designed in 1916.

◄◄ Using computer modelling to design a new car.

Design at work

Most designers try out their design by making a model. They check how it looks and whether it works.

A computer model is often cheaper to produce than a real model. The designer can see the product onscreen from different angles. The computer can even show the effects of different conditions – such as changing weather.

Logos

A logo is something that stands for a company or organization. It may be a picture, symbol or word. If the design is good, people will remember the logo.

The logo ►► for Apple Computers is an apple. Now it's silver, but it used to be stripy.

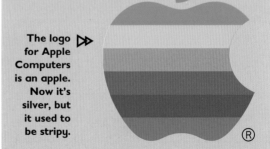

Clothes

Clothes cover your body and keep you warm. The clothes you wear depend on whether you are male or female, where you live, and what sort of life you lead.

In hot climates, people wear thin, light-coloured clothes because they are cooler. In cold climates, people wear layers of thick, cosy clothes.

Clothes around the world

Traditional dress means clothes worn by a particular people or in a particular place. The clothes have the same fabric, patterns and style.

In the Western world, styles change with the seasons. Most clothes are factory-made. Jeans and T-shirts are Western clothes that are popular everywhere.

India   Inuit, Canada   Masai, Kenya

◁◁ Some styles of traditional clothing from around the world.

Cameroon   Japan   Native American, Bolivia   Berber, Morocco

Work and play

Some people wear special clothes for work. Uniforms make police officers or supermarket staff easy to recognize. Other clothes are designed to protect workers. There are also special clothes for sports, such as swimsuits and football kits.

▽ Firefighters wear fire-resistant uniforms.

▽ This factory worker is using a sewing machine to make jeans.

Types of cloth

Cloth is woven from fibres (thin strands), usually by machine. Natural fibres include cotton and wool. Synthetic ones include nylon and Lycra. Cloth often contains a mix of natural and synthetic fibres.

Painting and sculpture

▽ This bronze sculpture was made by the Edo people of Benin, West Africa, in about 1550.

About 30,000 years ago prehistoric people were painting animals on cave walls. Since then people around the world have used art to decorate temples, palaces and even landscapes.

Painting and drawing are two art forms that we enjoy with our eyes. Other visual arts include pottery and sculpture.

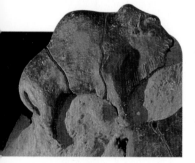

△ A clay figure of a bison sculpted in France around 20,000 years ago.

△ A painting on silk showing a tiger hunt in Rajasthan, northern India.

Sculpture

Sculptors work in many different materials, including metal, stone, wood and plastic. They carve or mould the material to give their sculpture its shape. Some modern sculptors weld or glue different objects and materials together.

Surfaces to paint on

Artists can paint on almost any surface, but most work on canvas, wood, paper or plaster (walls). Canvas is a rough cloth made of cotton. Painting on silk is popular in China and India. Most drawing is done on paper.

Paints

Artists use different kinds of paint, such as oils, watercolours or acrylics. The pigments that give paint its colour come from clays, rocks, metal ores, minerals and artificial dyes.

DID YOU KNOW?

The oldest known sculptures are small stone figures of women, made about 25,000 years ago.

Made to last?

Most art survives long after the artist who made it. But some artists deliberately create pieces that will not last. Navajo Indian sand paintings blow away. Ice sculptures melt. Large-scale works of art that are temporary are called installations. Artists take photos as a record.

Surrounded Islands (1980–1983), an installation ▷▷ by Christo (b 1935) and Jeanne-Claude (b 1935).

Art styles and artists

Most cultures have a long tradition of painting. China is known for its delicate landscape painting. Islamic art uses beautiful and intricate patterns, but very rarely shows things, people or animals.

In Western art, the individual artist is considered very important. Most famous artists are European.

Shaping tradition

Christianity has been a big influence on Western art. Many of the greatest paintings and sculptures were made for churches and cathedrals. They often show scenes from the Bible.

The art of ancient Greece and Rome has been important, too. During the Renaissance, which began in Italy in the 1300s, artists tried to learn from ancient art. They aimed to make their figures as beautiful and true to life as possible.

Child Holding a Dove by Pablo Picasso (1881–1973). Picasso was the most famous artist of the 20th century.

Swinging by Vassily Kandinsky, (1866–1944), one of the first abstract artists.

Rouen Cathedral by Claude Monet (1840–1926). Monet gives an impression of the building, rather than showing it realistically.

Abstract art

Abstract art describes paintings and sculptures that do not try to represent a real thing. Instead, they express an idea or a feeling. In abstract art, lines, colours, shapes, patterns and textures exist for their own sake.

Religions

A religion is a set of beliefs that a group of people follow. There are many different religions. The six main ones are Buddhism, Christianity, Hinduism, Islam, Judaism and Sikhism.

People who follow a religion usually worship a god or gods. They try to live a certain way.

Many gods

The oldest religions have many gods and goddesses. Hindus believe in a supreme force, called Brahman, that takes the form of different gods. Some of these are half-animal. The god Ganesh is part-elephant.

 Sikhism was founded by Guru Nanak, shown here with friends from other religions – Mardana, a Muslim (left), and Bala, a Hindu (right).

One god

Jews, Christians and Muslims worship a single God. They believe God sent prophets (messengers) to show them how to live. Christians follow the teachings of Jesus, who they believe was the Son of God. Muslims follow the teachings of Muhammad, who they believe was the last and greatest of God's prophets.

Belief systems

Not all religions mean worshipping a god. Buddhists follow the teachings of the Buddha and try to reach nirvana – perfect happiness, free from the worries of the world.

Jesus, whose teachings Christians follow.

Buddhist monks spend their time meditating (thinking deeply), studying and teaching.

KEY DATES

BC

c. 2000 Hinduism begins in India

c. 2000 Life of Abraham, father of Judaism

c. 500 Buddhism begins in India

AD

c. 30 Start of Christianity, following the death of Jesus

c. 610 Muhammad founds Islam in the Middle East

c. 1500 Sikhism begins in northern India

Holy books

Religious teachings are often written down in holy books. They may take the form of legends, histories, poems or laws. The Jewish holy book is called the Torah. The first five books of the Christian Old Testament make up the Torah.

The Torah ▷▷ (Jewish holy book) on a special stand.

Muslim children learning how to ▲ read the Koran in Arabic.

Worship

Holy buildings include temples (Hinduism and Buddhism), synagogues (Judaism), churches (Christianity), mosques (Islam) and gurdwaras (Sikhism). People visit these buildings to worship, pray, make offerings or study the holy books.

Muhammad is buried at this ▽ mosque in Medina, Saudi Arabia. ▽

Pilgrimage

A pilgrimage is a journey to a holy place. Thousands of Hindus travel to the holy River Ganges each year to bathe. The hajj is the pilgrimage to Mecca that every Muslim must make.

Hindu pilgrims ▽ in the Ganges. ▽

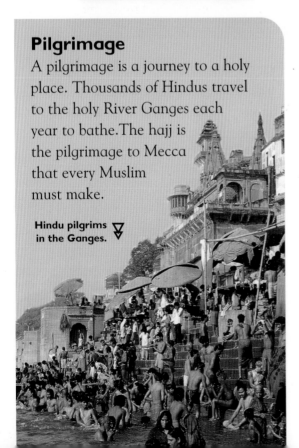

Signs of faith

Some people wear special clothes as a sign that they are part of a religion. Sikhs do not cut their hair.

In some religions, people follow a special diet. Jews call the food that they are allowed to eat kosher. Food that Muslims can eat is called halal.

Farming

Farming is growing crops and raising animals to provide food and other products. People first began to farm about 10,000 years ago.

Farms around the world are very different. Farmers grow crops and keep animals that are suited to their climate and land.

Farmers grow rice, a cereal crop, in flooded fields called paddies.

Growing crops

The most common crops are cereals, such as rice, wheat and maize. Tractors and other machines help farmers to produce as much grain as possible.

Farmers can use chemicals to improve the soil and to kill insect pests and weeds. Farming without chemicals is called organic farming.

Moving around

Farmers in the tropics grow crops such as maize, rice, manioc and millet. After about a year, the soil has given up all its goodness. The farmers move on and clear fresh land.

Farm animals

Some farmers use their land to grow crops and keep animals. This is called mixed farming.

Some farm animals are reared only for food. Others help with the work around the farm. Animals also provide skins (leather), wool or down (feathers).

This Masai woman from East Africa keeps cattle for meat, milk and leather.

DID YOU KNOW?

Most of the people who have ever lived have been farmers.

Farm animals were first bred from wild animals thousands of years ago.

wild boar

mouflon (wild sheep)

Fishing

Fishing is a very popular sport, but most fishers catch fish for food – to feed themselves or to sell.

Millions of people around the world work at catching, processing and selling fish.

The fishing industry

Some fishing boats stay near the coast and catch fish using rods and lines or small nets. They sail and return the same day.

Most of the world's fish catch comes from large, deep-sea fishing ships. They stay at sea for months.

Fishing for sport

Coarse fishing is the most popular type of sports fishing. You use a simple rod, a reel and line, hooks, weights, floats and bait (food to attract the fish).

Sea angling is like coarse fishing except that you catch fish from the sea.

Deep-sea fishing

There are three main ways big fishing boats catch fish – purse-seining, trawling and drift netting. In purse-seining, the net is open to begin with (1). It closes at the side (2) and bottom (3) to trap fish.

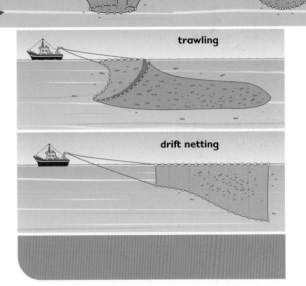

purse-seining

trawling

drift netting

▽ This man is fly-fishing. Fly-fishers catch fish you can eat, such as salmon or trout, and use hooks that look like flies.

DID YOU KNOW?

Fly-fishers use tinsel, wool, fur and feathers to hide their hooks.

119

Industry

Industry is the work that people do to produce goods or services. Farming, manufacturing and banking are different kinds of industry.

All industries belong to one of three groups. They are either a primary, secondary or service industry.

Primary industries

Industries that take natural materials from the Earth are known as primary industries. They include quarrying, mining, farming, forestry and fishing.

Quarry workers dig useful rock from the ground. This is a primary industry. ▽

Service industries

Some industries do not make a product. They offer a service instead. Transporting goods and selling them are two service industries. Other examples are banking, insurance, health care, education and tourism.

Trade unions

A trade union is a group of workers who campaign for better working conditions in their industry. If a union cannot reach an agreement with employers, its workers may go on strike (stop work).

▽ A march of trade union members in London, UK, in 1926.

Secondary industries

Industries that change natural materials into products are known as secondary industries. For example, the food-processing industry turns raw materials from farming and fishing into food products. Making clothes, cars or paper are other examples of secondary industries.

▽ Manufacturing is a secondary industry.

The Olympic Games

The Olympic Games are an international festival of sports that happen every four years. More than 200 countries take part, in over 270 events.

The Olympics are based on an ancient Greek festival, held at Olympia to honour the god Zeus. The modern Olympic Games started in summer 1896.

Where in the world?

The Olympics take place every four years at a different city – for example, Athens, Greece, in 2004; Beijing, China, in 2008; and London, UK, in 2012.

The Olympic flag's five rings represent the five continents (Africa, the Americas, Asia, Europe and Oceania) that take part in the games.

DID YOU KNOW?

Tug-of-war used to be one of the sporting events of the summer Olympics. It stopped in 1920.

Black athlete Jesse Owens won four gold medals at the 1936 Olympic Games, held in Berlin, Germany.

Sporting events

Olympic sports include athletics, gymnastics, swimming, judo, yacht racing, boxing, tennis, hockey and cycling.

For each event three medals are given out: gold for the winner, silver for second place and bronze for third.

Other sports festivals

Shortly after the Olympics there are the Paralympics, for disabled competitors. The Winter Olympics, for winter sports, takes place in the middle year between two summer Olympics.

Bobsleigh racing is a Winter Olympics sport.

Athletics

Winning a gold at the Olympics is every athlete's dream. There are over 40 athletics events in the Olympic Games.

Athletics includes track events, such as walking, running and hurdling, and field events, such as jumping and throwing.

US sprinter Michael Johnson winning the 200 metres at the Atlanta Olympics, 1996.

Running races

Running events on the track are divided into the sprints (100, 200 and 400 metres), middle-distance (800 and 1500 metres), and long-distance (5000 and 10,000 metres).

Relay races and hurdles are other track events.

Field events

The field events are split into jumps and throws. The jumps are the high jump, the pole vault, the long jump and the triple jump. The throws are the shot, discus, hammer and javelin.

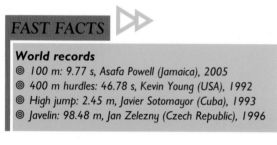

An athletics track.

110 m hurdles
100 m and 100 m hurdles
200 m
5000 m (12.5 laps)
water jump for steeplechase
home straight
finish line
shot
pole vault
long jump and triple jump
10,000 m (25 laps)
hammer and discus
high jump
javelin (runway)
3000 m steeplechase (7.5 laps)
800 m (2 laps)
400 m and 400 m hurdles (1 lap)
1500 m (3.75 laps)

For the high jump, the bar is raised after each round.

Football

There are several different games called football. Association football, or soccer, is the most popular. Others include rugby football and American football.

In soccer, only the goalkeeper can handle the ball. In rugby and American football, players can run holding the ball.

Soccer

A soccer match is played between two teams of 11 players and lasts for 90 minutes, with a 15-minute break between halves. The aim is to score goals by kicking or heading the ball into the opponents' goal.

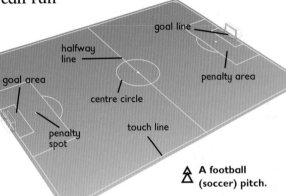

goal line

halfway line

goal area

centre circle

penalty area

penalty spot

touch line

A football (soccer) pitch.

American footballers wear padded clothing and helmets with face guards.

American football

American football is played between two teams of 11 players. Each game is made up of four 15-minute quarters. There are different ways to score points. Taking the ball across the goal line is called a touchdown and scores six points.

Rugby football

Rugby Union is the most widely played version of rugby. It is played between two teams of 15 players and lasts for 40 minutes each way. The aim is to score tries by touching the ball down behind the opponents' goal line.

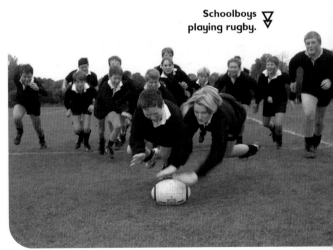

Schoolboys playing rugby.

Ball games

People have played ball games for thousands of years. Each has its own set of rules.

Some ball games, such as basketball and squash, are very energetic. Others, such as bowling or golf, are played at a slower pace.

Goal!

Many ball games are played by teams on a court or pitch with a goal at each end. Football (see page 123), basketball, hockey and polo are examples.

In basketball, players aim to throw the ball in their opponents' 'basket'. In hockey, players use sticks to hit the ball across the ground.

◄◄ The US basketball star, Michael Jordan.

Racket sports

Players of tennis, badminton and table tennis use a racket to hit the ball (or shuttlecock) to each other across a net. In squash the ball is bounced off the wall of the court instead.

△ Children playing baseball.

Bat and ball

In cricket, baseball and rounders, the two teams take turns to bat and bowl. The batters try to score runs. In baseball, this involves moving safely round the three bases and back to home plate.

▽ Martina Navratilova winning at Wimbledon, one of the top tennis tournaments.

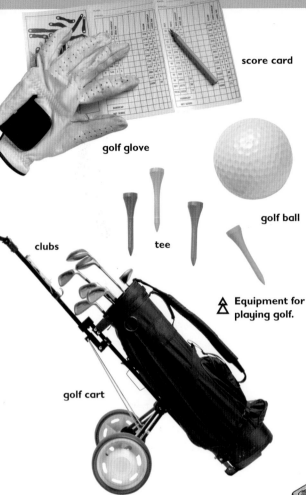

score card

golf glove

golf ball

clubs   tee

△ Equipment for playing golf.

golf cart

Golf

Golf is an outdoor game, played with sticks called clubs. Golf courses can be different lengths and shapes, but most have 18 'holes' – areas where players try to hit their ball into a hole in the ground. The aim is to complete each hole with as few hits as possible.

Bowling

There are many bowling games. At bowling alleys, players roll a large, heavy ball at a group of skittles or pins. The aim is to knock them over.

Lawn bowls, boules and bocce are all games where people try to throw their ball as close as possible to a smaller ball, known as the jack.

Table games

Billiards, snooker and pool are table games. Players use a stick, called a cue, to knock balls into the pockets around the edge of the table. Depending on the game, there are different numbers of balls of different colours.

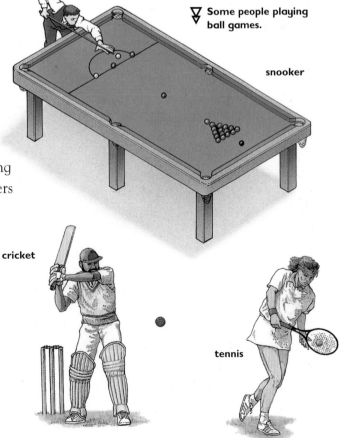

▽ Some people playing ball games.

snooker

cricket

tennis

DID YOU KNOW?

The Olmecs, who lived in Mexico from around 1200 BC, played ball as a way of worshipping their gods. The Maya and the Aztecs also played ritual ball games.

Water sports

There are many different sports that happen in or on water. Some take place in swimming pools. Others are enjoyed outside, on rivers and lakes or at sea.

Water sports such as swimming and rowing rely on muscle power. In others, such as sailing and surfing, people use the power of the wind or waves.

Pool sports

In competitive swimming, there are races for freestyle (front crawl), breast-stroke, backstroke and butterfly. There are also relay races and medley races (where swimmers use a different stroke for each stage of the race).

Diving is entering the water head first with as little splash as possible. The dive is marked by judges.

Many people learn to swim as children.

 FAST FACTS

- Between 1936 and 1942 Danish swimmer Ragnhild Hveger set 42 swimming world records.
- At Waimea Bay, Hawaii, USA, surfers ride waves that are 9–11 m high.
- In 1986 100 water skiers were towed behind one boat at Queensland, Australia.

A surfer rides a wave to shore.

Windsurfers do jumps or other stunts.

Surfing and windsurfing

Surfing is the sport of riding a surfboard towards the shore on the face of a wave. Surfboards are made of hard, light plastic foam, covered with resin and fibreglass.

Windsurfing is a bit like surfing but the board has a sail. The windsurfer steers by moving the sail.

Canoeing

There are two types of racing canoe. The Canadian canoe has a single-bladed paddle, which is used first on one side, then on the other. The kayak has a two-bladed paddle.

Some canoe races are held on still water. Others are on rough, rocky courses.

◀◀ Canoeing over a rough course like this is called white-water racing.

Rowing

Rowing boats are narrow, light and streamlined. The rowers use long paddles called oars.

Rowing boats have crews of one, two, four or eight oarsmen. Eights have an extra person called a cox who steers the boat.

Sailing

⋀⋀ A two-person rowing boat.

Racing yachts range from one-person dinghies to ocean-going vessels that need a crew of 20 or more.

Racing takes place both inshore (close to the coast) and offshore (out at sea). Boat races are called regattas.

▽ A sailing dinghy.

Motor-powered sports

Powerboats are racing boats with engines. The fastest ones zip along at more than 240 km per hour. Motorboats are also used to tow water-skiers. Water-skiers compete in slaloms, where they weave between obstacles, or they perform tricks and stunts.

A water-skier seen ▽ from the air. ▽

Winter sports

Winter sports take place on ice or snow. Skiing and ice skating are the most popular. Other winter sports include snowboarding, tobogganing, ice yachting and even dog-sled racing.

The main competition for winter sports is the Winter Olympics.

Speed skaters wear protective ▷▷
helmets and padding.

Skating

Speed skaters try to skate a certain distance as fast as possible. Figure skaters perform a routine to music and judges give them marks out of 10 for their moves.

Many people skate for fun, too, on ice rinks and frozen lakes or rivers.

Skis and boards

Skiing and snowboarding are mountain sports. Skiers wear a runner (ski) on each foot. Snowboarders balance on a board.

In Alpine skiing competitors race down the slopes. Nordic skiing includes cross-country racing and ski-jumping.

◁◁ Freestyle snowboarders perform
tricks on their snowboard.

Snow transport

Sleds are vehicles with runners instead of wheels. Toboggans are sleds that people ride for fun. Bobsleighs are racing sleds.

Dog-sleds are also used for racing, but sometimes they carry out serious work, transporting people or supplies.

Skiing for ▷▷
fun in a
mountain
resort.

DID YOU KNOW?

An ice-yacht is a boat on skis. In 1938 John Buckstaff (USA) raced his ice-yacht at speeds of 230 km/h on frozen Lake Winnebago, Wisconsin, USA.

Martial arts

Martial arts are sports that allow people to practise fighting skills.

Karate, tae kwon do, kendo and judo are all martial arts from East Asia. Boxing and wrestling have been around in Europe for thousands of years.

Target sports

Archery and shooting are called target sports, because they involve firing weapons at a target.

An archery ▷▷ target.

▽▽ A women's judo contest at the Olympic Games.

Punches and kicks

In boxing, contestants fight with their fists. Kick-boxing and karate involve kicks as well as punches.

Kung fu is the name for many different Chinese martial arts, including shaolin, wing chun and drunken boxing. The famous martial artist Bruce Lee studied wing chun.

Ways to wrestle

Wrestling involves grappling an opponent and throwing him or her to the ground. Sumo and judo, both from Japan, are very different styles of wrestling.

People who practise judo wear a coloured belt to show how skilled they are. Black belt is the highest rank.

◁◁ The fencer to score most touches wins the contest.

△ Sumo wrestlers follow a special diet and are not allowed to cut their hair.

Using weapons

Fencing is an ancient combat sport where people use swords – and wear padded clothing. In Japanese fencing, or kendo, the swords are made of bamboo.

Timeline of world history

	ASIA	AMERICAS AND OCEANIA	AFRICA AND MIDDLE EAST	EUROPE
Before 10,000 BC	• Hunter-gatherers • Stone tools used – knives, axes and harpoons	• Hunter-gatherers • Cave art in Australia from 40,000 BC	• First humans • From 100,000 BC people spread through all continents	• Hunter-gatherers • Cave paintings from 30,000 BC • Female figurines made
10,000 BC	• Rice and millet farming • Pottery made in Japan and China	• Hunter-gatherers • Canoes and sledges	• Cereal farming • Wheel invented • Cattle, sheep and goats domesticated	• Farming from 7000 BC • Canoes and sledges • Animals domesticated and herded
5000 BC	• Horses domesticated • Cities in China • Silk-weaving in China	• Maize (corn) farmed in Mexico • Pottery made in South America • Llamas domesticated	An early plough. • Plough invented • Bronze and pottery made • Writing invented	Stonehenge, Britain. • Standing stones • Flint mines • Farming spreads and ploughs used
2500 BC	• Indus Valley civilization • Aryans invade northern India • Beginnings of Hinduism	A Pacific islander's canoe. • Settlers reach Pacific Islands • Temples built in Peru • Cotton grown in Peru	An Egyptian pyramid. • Pyramids built in Egypt • Sumer civilization • Beginnings of Judaism	• Bronze objects made • Minoan civilization • Mycenean civilization A burial mask from Mycenae.
1000 BC	• Zhou dynasty in China • Taoism founded • Confucius (Kongzi) and Buddha lived	• Settlements in Polynesia • Chavin culture in Peru • Olmec civilization in Mexico An Olmec stone head.	• Kingdom of Kush in East Africa • Assyrian empire • Persian empire	• Celts move into Germany and France • Greek city states • Hillforts in western Europe
500 BC	• Mauryan empire in India • Qin dynasty unifies China • Great Silk Road opens	• Teotihuacán built • Early Maya culture • Hieroglyphic writing in Mexico Mayan stone carving.	• Nok culture in Nigeria • Alexander the Great conquers Persia • Romans conquer Syria, Palestine and Egypt	• Great age of Athens • Alexander the Great conquers Greece • Growth of Roman empire
AD 1	Terracotta horse. • Buddhism reaches China and South-east Asia • Paper invented in China • Emperors in Japan	• Huge stone temples built in Peru	• Jews expelled from Jerusalem • Birth of Christianity • Kingdom of Axum, Ethiopia	• Roman empire at its height The Colosseum, Rome.
AD 250 AD 499	• Gupta empire in India • Horse-collar harness first used in China	• Nazca civilization in southern Peru	• Byzantine empire A Byzantine madonna and child.	• Christianity spreads • Frankish kingdom founded

ASIA

AD 500	• Tang dynasty in China • Buddhism established in Japan
AD 750	• Fujiwara family controls Japan • Printing and gunpowder in China

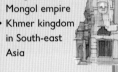

A Khmer temple.

1000	• Genghis Khan's Mongol empire • Khmer kingdom in South-east Asia
1250	• Yuan (Mongol) and Ming dynasties in China • Conquests of Timur • Growth of Vietnam
1500	• Beginnings of Sikhism • Qing (Manzhou) dynasty in China • Tokugawa shoguns in Japan
1700	• Qing dynasty • Decline of Mughal empire • British control India
1800	• Europeans control trade in Asia • Opium Wars in China
1900	• China becomes a communist state • Indian independence • World War II • Vietnam War
Present day	

AMERICAS AND OCEANIA

• Maya civilization at its height

A Mayan temple.

• Toltec civilization in Mexico

• Vikings sail to North America
• Polynesians settle in Hawaii, New Zealand and Easter Island

• Aztec and Inca empires at their height
• Columbus reaches America

• Spanish conquer Aztecs and Incas
• European colonies in the Americas
• Slavery grows

The first US flag.
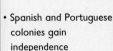
• USA gains independence
• European settlers in Australia

• Spanish and Portuguese colonies gain independence
• American Civil War

• USA becomes a superpower
• Moon landing
• Technological revolution

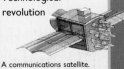

A communications satellite.

AFRICA AND MIDDLE EAST

A mosque in Persia.

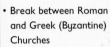

• Muhammad founds Islam
• Sassanid (Persian) empire

• Abbasid empire
• Empire of Ghana, West Africa
• Great Zimbabwe, East Africa

• Saladin defeats Christian crusaders
• Turks conquer Palestine

• Mongols overthrow Abbasids
• Empires of Benin and Mali in West Africa
• Black Death

A bronze head from Benin.

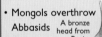

• Ottoman (Turkish) empire at its height
• Dutch settlers in South Africa

• Slave trade grows
• Ottoman decline
• Asante kingdom in West Africa

A gold Asante statue.

• Slave trade ends
• Africa divided into European colonies

• Independent African and Arab states
• Israel founded
• Two Gulf Wars

EUROPE

• Gregory the Great establishes the power of the pope
• Muslims conquer Spain

A Viking longboat.

• Viking raids and settlement
• Empire of Charlemagne

• Break between Roman and Greek (Byzantine) Churches
• Normans conquer England and Sicily

• Ottoman Turks capture Constantinople
• Black Death
• Renaissance begins

• Reformation (Protestants split from Catholic Church)
• Ottomans invade central Europe

• England and Scotland united
• French Revolution
• Start of Industrial Revolution

A steam locomotive.

• Napoleonic wars
• Italy united
• Germany united

• World Wars I and II
• Russian Revolution
• European Union founded

Ancient peoples

Early people moved around, hunting and gathering wild foods. As people discovered how to farm, they started to build settlements.

Civilizations sprang up – societies with government, religion and even writing. The best known were in Mesopotamia (now Iraq), Egypt, Greece and Italy (Rome), but there were many others.

Law

King Hammurabi of Babylon was one of the earliest rulers to write down his laws. They were carved into a stone called the Code of Hammurabi.

The Code of ▷▷ Hammurabi (c. 1780 BC).

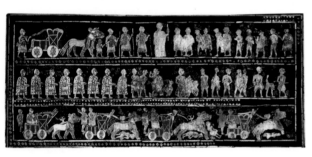

△ This carving shows Sumerian soldiers coming home from a war.

Mesopotamia

The Sumerians established the first civilization in Mesopotamia around 3500 BC. The Babylonians took control there from around 1790 BC. Both peoples built stepped towers called ziggurats.

▽ Some ancient civilizations and cities.

Key

Sumerians (about 3500 to 200 BC)

Egyptians (about 3100 to 30 BC)

Indus Valley civilization (about 2500 to 1600 BC)

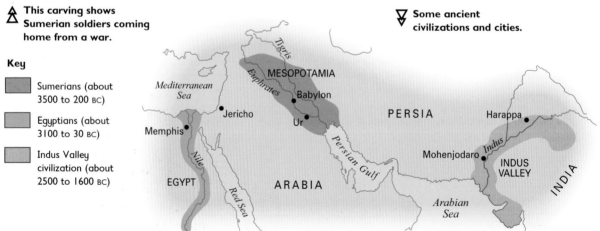

Mediterranean Sea · Jericho · Memphis · Babylon · Ur · MESOPOTAMIA · Tigris · Euphrates · PERSIA · Harappa · Mohenjodaro · Indus · INDUS VALLEY · INDIA · Persian Gulf · EGYPT · Nile · Red Sea · ARABIA · Arabian Sea

India and China

The Indus Valley civilization started around 2500 BC in what is now Pakistan. One of its largest cities, Mohenjodaro, had broad streets and houses with bathrooms.

The first Chinese civilization grew up in about 1500 BC. Its people, the Shang, used a type of picture writing.

DID YOU KNOW?

Most civilizations grew up alongside rivers, where there was water for people's crops.

Ancient Egyptians

The Egyptians built up one of the most amazing civilizations of the ancient world. It lasted almost 3000 years (from about 3200 BC to 340 BC).

Today, people are still dazzled by Egyptian art and buildings, especially the famous pyramids.

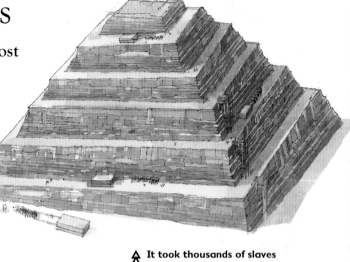

△ It took thousands of slaves years to build a large pyramid.

The Nile

The Egyptians depended on the River Nile. Most ordinary Egyptians farmed land near the river. They dug channels to bring water to their fields.

The Nile was also the Egyptians' main highway and it provided fish to eat.

△ A tomb painting showing a nobleman hunting river birds by the Nile.

The pharaoh

Egypt was ruled by a royal family, or dynasty. The pharaoh was head of the family. Most pharaohs were men. A pharaoh had enormous power. The Egyptians thought that he was the god Horus on Earth.

KEY DATES

BC
c. 3050	Egypt unites under one pharaoh
c. 3000	Hieroglyphic writing appears
c. 2650	Worship of Sun god Ra begins
c. 2465	The pyramids and sphinx at Giza are complete
305–30	Greeks rule Egypt and move the capital to Alexandria
30	Egypt becomes part of the Roman empire

The Egyptians had a kind of picture writing (hieroglyphs). ▽
This spells the name of Pharaoh Cleopatra.

Religion

The Egyptians worshipped more than 750 gods. There were Sun gods and crop gods, gods of love and war, gods in human form and animal form, and several gods that were half-human, half-animal.

From left to right: Anubis, Isis, Osiris and Ra.

Egyptian gods

Jackal-headed Anubis was the god of tombs. Isis was the goddess of magic and mother of Horus, the sky god. Her husband, Osiris, ruled the underworld. The Egyptians' most important god was the Sun god, Ra, who had the head of a falcon.

The Egyptians made animal mummies, not just human ones.

The underworld

The Egyptians believed that after they died they went to live in the underworld. They thought they would need their bodies there. They learned how to preserve bodies as mummies that did not rot. People were buried with things that they might need in the next life, such as food and clothes.

Royal tombs

Important Egyptians were buried in magnificent tombs. Some royal tombs were enormous stone pyramids. Others were underground chambers cut into solid rock.

In AD 1922, the tomb of a young pharaoh called Tutankhamun was discovered. Parts of the tomb had been robbed, but it still contained amazing treasures.

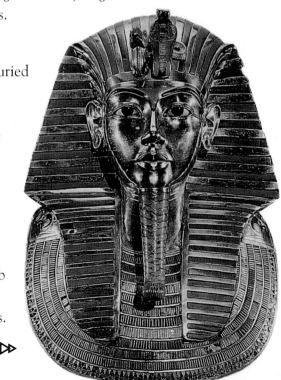

The golden death mask of Pharaoh Tutankhamun (c. 1370–1352 BC).

Ancient Greeks

The Greeks created Europe's first major civilization. It lasted from around 800 BC until around 150 BC.

Today we still admire Greek ideas and discoveries. And most countries are ruled by a government, just as ancient Athens was.

Two of the greatest ancient Greek thinkers were Plato (left) and Aristotle (right).

Earlier civilizations

There were two earlier Greek civilizations: the Minoans on Crete (from around 2000 BC) and the Mycenaeans (from around 1600 BC). Both peoples built fine palaces and wrote an early form of Greek. They had disappeared by 1100 BC.

City states

Ancient Greece was divided into city states, made up of a city and the land around it. Each city state had its own government and laws. Athens and Sparta were the most important city states.

The golden age

In the 400s BC Athens grew rich from trade. Craftspeople made beautiful pottery and poets wrote wonderful plays. Architects built temples on the Acropolis, a hill overlooking the city.

How the Acropolis may have looked around 450 BC.

A painted vase showing the Greek hero Theseus killing a monster called the Minotaur.

Alexander the Great ruled from 336 to 323 BC. After his death, his empire fell apart.

Alexander the Great

In the 300s BC, Alexander the Great spread Greek ideas across Asia. By the 100s BC, Greece was under Roman rule. The Romans adopted many Greek ideas and even some of their gods.

Key

1 holy place of Zeus
2 Parthenon (temple of the goddess Athene)
3 theatre of the god Dionysus
4 temple of Athene and the god Poseidon
5 statue of Athene
6 holy place of the goddess Artemis
7 gateway

Romans

The Romans were an ancient people who created a huge empire, with its capital at Rome. By the AD 100s the Roman empire surrounded the Mediterranean and stretched from Britain to Syria.

Paved stone roads connected all parts of the empire. Wherever they went, the Romans took their way of life and their language, Latin.

The army

The Roman army helped to make the empire. It conquered peoples, built forts and roads, and kept Roman lands safe from attack.

Foot soldiers were organized into legions of about 5000 men. Each soldier carried two javelins for throwing, and a sword and a shield for close fighting. Other units, called cavalry, fought on horseback.

▽ **All Roman towns had public baths where people went to relax and meet friends.**

The provinces

The Romans divided the lands they conquered into areas called provinces. They encouraged the locals to live like Romans, and built temples to Roman gods.

Everyday life

Roman towns were well planned, with a central meeting place called the forum. Most people lived in apartments above shops or workshops. Richer people had houses with gardens and underfloor heating. Pipes brought water to houses, businesses, fountains and public baths.

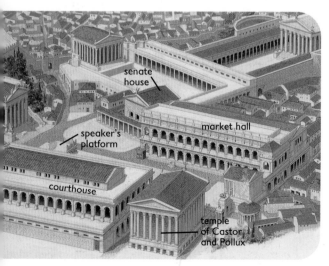

senate house
speaker's platform
market hall
courthouse
temple of Castor and Pollux

The forum in the centre of Rome was made up of temples and government buildings. △

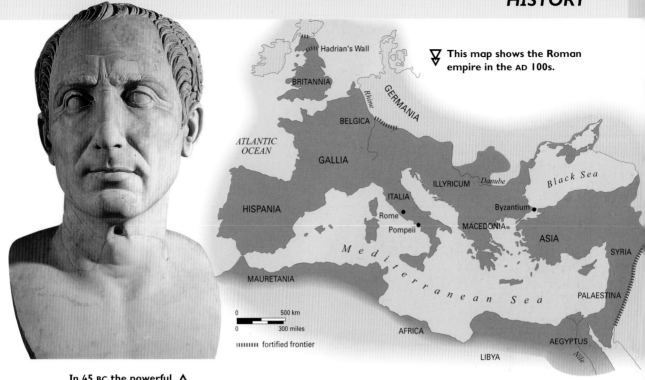

This map shows the Roman empire in the AD 100s.

In 45 BC the powerful general Julius Caesar made himself ruler of Rome.

From republic to empire

At first Rome was a republic. At the head were two men, called consuls. A sort of parliament, called the senate, made new laws.

In 27 BC, Octavius, the adopted son of Julius Caesar, made himself emperor. He took the name Augustus. The next two centuries were the most peaceful time in Rome's history.

The end of the empire

From the AD 200s, weak emperors left the Roman empire open to attack. In AD 330 the Emperor Constantine moved the capital east to Byzantium (now Istanbul in Turkey). The western part of the empire was gradually invaded by northern tribes, and in 410 Rome fell. The eastern part became the Byzantine empire.

The Byzantine empire

The Byzantine empire was at its height in the AD 500s when the Emperor Justinian conquered Egypt and parts of Italy, Spain and North Africa. Much of the empire fell to Muslim Arabs in the 700s and 800s. The city of Constantinople was captured by the Ottoman Turks in 1453.

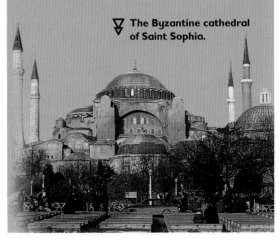

The Byzantine cathedral of Saint Sophia.

Incas

The Incas built an empire in and around the Andes mountains. They had no iron tools, but they were excellent builders. Their network of roads stretched for 20,000 kilometres.

Spanish conquerors destroyed the Inca empire in the 1500s.

SOUTH AMERICA

Inca empire

● Machu Picchu

The Inca ▷▷ empire in the early 1500s.

Building an empire

Warlike Incas came to Cuzco in Peru around AD 1000. Over the next 500 years, they built up an empire that stretched along the west coast of South America.

DID YOU KNOW?

Just before the Spanish conquest, the Inca empire had about 12 million people.

The Incas ▷▷
killed this
young girl and
buried her
high in the
mountains, as
an offering to
the gods.

Inca society

Most ordinary Incas were farmers. They grew maize (corn), tomatoes and peanuts, and used channels to water their fields. Their ruler was known as the Inca. He said that the Sun was his ancestor (an earlier member of his family). Everyone had to obey him.

Machu Picchu

The Incas built the city of Machu Picchu on a high mountain ridge. It had a palace and many temples. Some experts think it was a holiday town for Inca nobles.

The city of ▷▷
Machu Picchu.

Middle Ages

The Middle Ages is the time in European history from the end of the Roman empire (about AD 450) until 1500. During the first 500 years tribes struggled for power.

Gradually, Europe settled down. Many of today's countries appeared.

Christendom

The Roman Catholic Church was the most powerful force in Europe. Everyone went to church on Sundays and 'holy days'. Wherever you were, the service was in Latin (the language of ancient Rome).

KEY DATES

711	Moors (Muslims) invade Spain
800	Charlemagne is crowned Emperor of the West
1066	Norman Conquest of England
1236	Mongols invade Russia
1348	Black Death (plague) reaches Europe
1450s	Printing used in Europe
1469	Spain ruled under one crown

Key

■ western Christendom

■ eastern Christendom

■ Muslim lands

➡ Mongol invaders

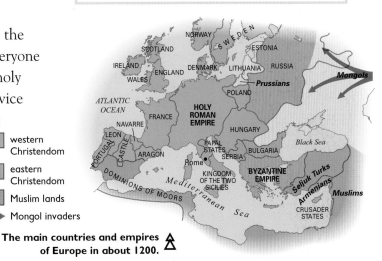

The main countries and empires of Europe in about 1200.

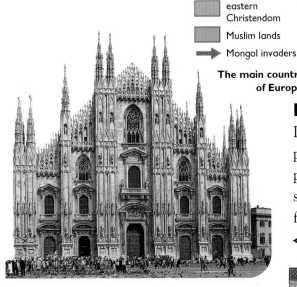

◀◀ The Roman Catholic Church put up many fine buildings such as Milan Cathedral, Italy.

Daily life

Peasants could not read or write and were desperately poor. People lived short lives, and diseases such as the Black Death meant that death was never far away.

Kings, knights and peasants

In the Middle Ages, everyone had their place. The king was at the top and the peasants were at the bottom. Everyone served the person above them, in return for land and protection.

Burying plague victims. The Black ▶▶ Death reached Europe in 1348.

Knights and castles

Knights were noblemen who fought on horseback. In medieval Europe it was a great honour to be a knight.

Knights served the king. In return, he gave them lands. Many knights lived in castles – strong buildings that could withstand attack. Other knights served lords who lived in castles.

Knightly equipment

Each knight paid for his own armour and warhorse. The steel armour protected the knight from head to toe. Knights carried a sword, a shield and sometimes a long, heavy lance. Knights became less important on the battlefield after the invention of guns.

Heraldry

Each knight wore a 'coat of arms' – a design on his shield. This meant he could be recognized easily in battle.

The background colour of the shield was called its field. The field was split up into divisions or it had a picture or shape, called a charge.

Duke William of Normandy and his knights before the battle of Hastings, where they defeated the English.

Divisions

quarterly

paly

Charges

chevron

bend

fess

saltire

Jousting tournaments

Jousting was a sport for knights. The tournament was a mock battle that allowed knights to show off their fighting skills.

Jousting knights fought with blunt lances but they could still be injured or killed.

Knightly behaviour

Knights followed a set of rules. A knight had to be brave but kind to the weak (especially women), strong but polite, determined but honest.

Early castles

Motte-and-bailey castles were built all over western Europe from the 900s. They had a wooden tower (the keep) built on a high mound (the motte), with a fenced area (the bailey) at the foot of the mound.

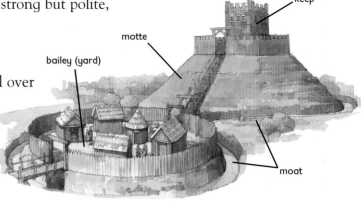

▽ A wooden motte-and-bailey castle.

keep

motte

bailey (yard)

moat

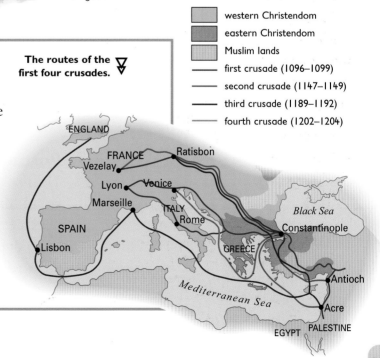

lord's living area

great hall

keep

battlements

kitchen

guardroom

outer walls

storerooms

gardens

church

moat

dungeon

drawbridge

tower

Walls of stone

From the 1100s, castles were rebuilt in stone. The tops of the walls were called battlements. Defenders could fire arrows through slits in the battlements. Castles also had a drawbridge that could be raised at the first sign of attack.

◀◀ A cut-away view of a stone castle.

The crusades

The crusades were eight wars that were fought after the pope asked Christian soldiers to drive Muslims from the lands mentioned in the Bible. Kings, knights and many ordinary people took part. When the crusades ended, all of the Holy Land was in Muslim hands.

The routes of the first four crusades. ▽

Key

	western Christendom
	eastern Christendom
	Muslim lands

— first crusade (1096–1099)
— second crusade (1147–1149)
— third crusade (1189–1192)
— fourth crusade (1202–1204)

ENGLAND

FRANCE

Ratisbon

Vezelay

Lyon

Venice

Marseille

ITALY

Rome

Black Sea

Constantinople

SPAIN

GREECE

Lisbon

Antioch

Mediterranean Sea

Acre

EGYPT

PALESTINE

Explorers and exploration

The period between 1450 and 1650 is sometimes called the Age of Exploration. During this time, European explorers travelled around the world, discovering different lands and peoples.

Europe and Asia had traded since ancient times. But goods had been passed from merchant to merchant, so no one had made the whole journey.

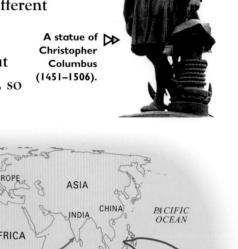

A statue of ▷▷ Christopher Columbus (1451–1506).

Key

→ Bartholomeu Dias (1488)

→ Christopher Columbus (1492)

→ John Cabot (1497)

→ Vasco da Gama (1497–1499)

→ Ferdinand Magellan and Juan Sebastián Elcano (1519–1522)

The main European ▷▷ voyages of discovery.

KEY DATES

1275 Marco Polo reaches China

1332 Ibn Batuta reaches India

1405 Cheng Ho begins his travels around the Indian Ocean

1488 Dias sails round the southern tip of Africa

1492 Columbus reaches the West Indies

1498 Da Gama reaches India

1519 Magellan sets out to sail around the world

1553 Search for the North-west Passage begins

1642 Tasman reaches Tasmania and New Zealand

Early explorers

In the 1200s Marco Polo travelled from Italy to China. In the 1300s the Arab explorer Ibn Batuta journeyed through the Middle East and on to India. And in the early 1400s the Chinese explorer Cheng Ho sailed to Persia, Arabia and down the coast of Africa.

Portuguese explorers

The Portuguese wanted to find a sea route round Africa to India. In 1488 Bartholomeu Dias reached the Cape of Good Hope. Ten years later Vasco da Gama continued across the ocean to India.

Before long, Portuguese sailors had pressed on to China and Japan.

America

The Vikings reached North America 1000 years ago, but their voyages were forgotten. In 1492, Christopher Columbus crossed the Atlantic looking for a way to China. Instead, he reached the West Indies.

The newly discovered continent was named after Amerigo Vespucci, who explored South America.

⚠ The fleet of the Dutch explorer William Barents, who died trying to find the North-west Passage.

Pirates

In the Age of Exploration there were more ships on the seas – and many carried treasure. Pirates were sea-robbers. Not all were after gold. Muslim corsairs attacked ships off North Africa and captured Christian slaves.

Some pirates, such as Blackbeard (Edward Teach), grew famous for their terrible cruelty. Most pirates were men, but a few were women.

▽ A Muslim corsair.

North-west Passage

French, Dutch and British explorers tried to sail round North America. They failed because this North-west Passage is frozen solid. Sailors also failed to find a North-east Passage, round Asia.

Captain ▷▷ James Cook (1728–1779) claimed New Zealand and Australia for Britain.

Later explorers

By 1650, people had mapped an outline of the continents. The details were filled in over the next 250 years.

James Cook explored the Pacific. Lewis and Clarke crossed North America. Mungo Park, David Livingstone, Henry Stanley and others explored Africa. In the early 20th century, explorers reached the North and South Poles.

Vikings

The Vikings were Norse peoples who lived in the Scandinavian countries of Norway, Denmark and Sweden.

From the 700s, Vikings left their homes in search of land. They made raids across the seas and settled in other countries. Vikings were also successful traders.

Country life

Most Vikings were peaceful farmers. They grew wheat, oats, barley and vegetables and they kept cattle, sheep, pigs and chickens.

The centre of every Viking village was the great hall. Here Viking men and women feasted and told fantastic stories of gods and heroes.

This Viking ice-skate was found at York, England. It is made of leather and animal bone.

Towns and trade

In towns, craftspeople made clothes, jewellery, tools and weapons. Merchants traded these goods abroad. They brought back ivory and furs from Iceland, silk and spices from Baghdad, and slaves and furs from Russia.

Viking raids

Viking invaders first hit Britain around AD 793. Raiders took treasure, and slaves to work on their farms. Vikings also settled across northern Europe and as far west as Greenland and North America.

Viking ships

A Viking longship, built for raiding, could carry 200 fighting men. The Vikings built wider, deeper ships called *knarrs* for trade, and little rowing boats called *faerings*. Ships had both oars and sails.

Key
1	sail	4	side rudder	7	shields
2	figurehead	5	deck	8	mast
3	keel	6	hull		

A Viking longship.

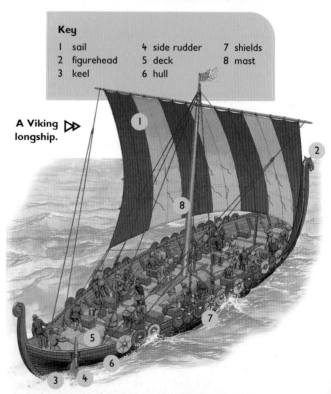

Aztecs

For almost 200 years the Aztecs ruled an area that is now part of Mexico. Their empire ended in 1519 when the Spanish arrived.

The Aztecs were great builders and fine craftworkers, but their civilization was also extremely bloodthirsty.

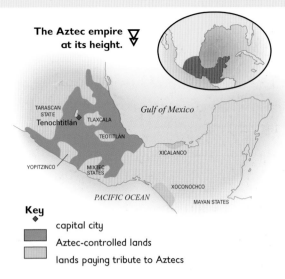

The Aztec empire at its height.

Key

◆ capital city

Aztec-controlled lands

lands paying tribute to Aztecs

▽ **The Aztecs built their temples on top of huge, stepped pyramids.**

Capital city

The Aztecs came to central Mexico around 1345. They built a huge city on an island in Lake Texcoco. They called it Tenochtitlán (now Mexico City). The Aztec emperor, his courtiers and his priests lived here.

Worship

The Aztecs worshipped many gods. The Sun god was called Huitzilopochtli. Aztec priests sacrificed live animals and people to this god. They cut out their victims' hearts while they were still beating.

DID YOU KNOW?

The Aztecs did not have money. They traded feathers and cacao beans instead.

End of the Aztecs

The Spanish conqueror Hernán Cortés defeated the Aztecs. His army had horses, guns and metal weapons. Some of the Aztecs believed that Cortés was the feathered serpent god, Quetzalcoatl.

▽ **An archaeologist working at an Aztec burial site in Teotihuacán, Mexico.**

Great empires

The age of empire was the time when European countries controlled land on other continents – Asia, Africa and the Americas. This period lasted from the 1500s until the 1900s.

Earlier great empires included those of the Mongols and the Ottoman Turks.

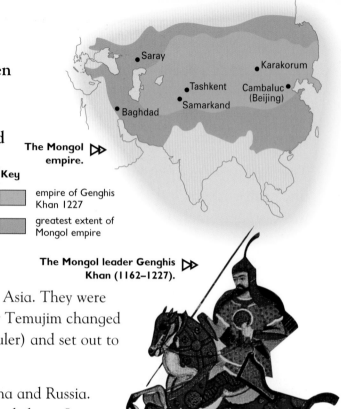

The Mongol ▷▷ empire.

Key

▢ empire of Genghis Khan 1227

▢ greatest extent of Mongol empire

The Mongol leader Genghis ▷▷ Khan (1162–1227).

Genghis Khan

The Mongols were a people from central Asia. They were excellent horsemen. In 1206, their leader Temujim changed his name to Genghis Khan (Universal Ruler) and set out to conquer the world.

Genghis's armies conquered parts of China and Russia. After his death, the Mongol empire expanded into Iran (Persia), Iraq and Europe.

Timur

The Mongols were driven from China in 1368. They found a new warrior leader, Timur the Lame (or Tamerlane). Timur took Northern India and defeated the Ottoman Turks, but his empire collapsed after his death.

Ottoman empire

The Ottoman (Turkish) empire lasted for 600 years. It was named after its first sultan (ruler), Uthman I (1258–1326). The Ottoman capital was Constantinople (Istanbul).

Sulieman the Magnificent (1494–1566) expanded the Ottoman empire into Hungary and Iraq. He also encouraged poetry, art and fine buildings.

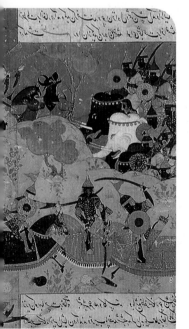

△ Timur's army invading India in 1398.

Suleiman the Magnificent ruled from 1520 to 1566 – longer than any other Ottoman sultan. ▽▽

Europeans in the Americas

Spain and Portugal were the first European nations to conquer empires – in South and Central America. In the 1600s the British, French and Dutch set up colonies in North America.

From colonies to independence

Europeans settled in the American colonies. They brought in slaves from Africa to do the hard work. In the late 1700s and early 1800s colonies rebelled. Countries including the United States, Brazil, Mexico and Argentina were born.

△ A Spanish gold mine at Cerro Rico in South America during the 1700s.

South African Zulu ▷▷
warriors fighting the
British in 1879. Almost all
of their land was taken.

The rest of the world

Europe had founded colonies elsewhere. Britain claimed Australia and New Zealand, India and Malaya. The French took Indo-China (Cambodia and Vietnam).

Africa suffered most. The Europeans carved up most of the continent. Sometimes countries took lands simply to stop other countries getting them.

▽ The main European empires in the Americas (around 1750) and in the rest of the world (around 1900).

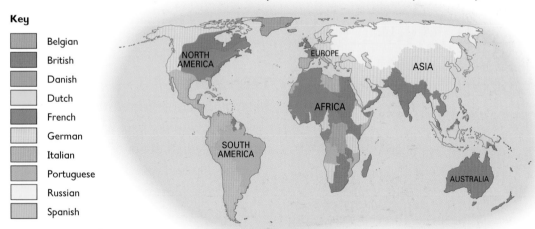

Key

- Belgian
- British
- Danish
- Dutch
- French
- German
- Italian
- Portuguese
- Russian
- Spanish

End of empire

By 1945 some colonies, such as Australia, already governed themselves. Starting with India, all Europe's remaining colonies became independent. In 1997 Britain handed Hong Kong back to China and the age of empire was over.

Inventions and inventors

An inventor is someone who makes something new or who finds new ways of using old ideas. What he or she makes is called an invention.

Throughout history, humans have moved forwards because of inventors and their inventions.

Then and now

Some inventions are so old that no one knows who invented them. They include axes, ploughs and knives. They may have appeared in different parts of the world at different times.

Some inventions are named after their inventor. Examples include Biro pens, Hoover vacuum cleaners and Diesel engines. Most modern inventions are too complicated to be invented by one person.

DID YOU KNOW?

American inventor Thomas Edison (1847–1931) came up with more than 1000 inventions in his lifetime.

▽ **Polynesian children fishing from their canoe.**

Birth of science

Between about 1500 and 1700 European thinkers came up with a new, scientific way of thinking about things. This was helped along by new inventions.

Galileo Galilei (1564–1642) adapted the telescope and was the first to use it to look into space. Robert Hooke (1635–1703) invented a powerful microscope.

A drawing of Robert Hooke's microscope. ▽

Transport

Some of the earliest inventions made it easier for humans to get around. Dugout canoes appeared about 8000 years ago. Once people had invented the wheel, around 5500 years ago, they developed chariots, carts and other forms of transport.

In the last century many new forms of transport were invented, including tanks, rockets, jet planes, helicopters, hovercraft and spacecraft.

Factory machines

Inventions often make it easier for people to do jobs. From around 1750, new inventions such as spinning frames, weaving machines and steam engines appeared. These allowed people to make goods quickly and cheaply in factories. This change began in Britain but soon spread to the rest of the world. It was called the Industrial Revolution.

Richard Arkwright's ▷▷ spinning frame, invented in 1769.

◁◁ Alexander Graham Bell, who invented the telephone in 1876.

Communications

The telephone was invented by Alexander Graham Bell (1847–1922) in 1876. Computers, satellites and the Internet have all appeared in the last 100 years. These inventions help people to communicate. The Internet even has websites and chatrooms where inventors swap ideas!

▽ ENIAC, built in the 1940s, was one of the earliest computers.

Satellites in ▷▷ space do many jobs. This one helps people to navigate (find the way) on Earth.

Dolly the Sheep. ▽

The secret of life

Can an animal be an invention? Dolly the Sheep was born in 1996. Instead of developing from an egg cell, she was copied (cloned) from an adult sheep's cell. Dolly was the first mammal that scientists managed to clone.

American Revolution

Before the American Revolution, America was made up of colonies that were ruled by the British king – from nearly 5000 kilometres across the ocean.

The colonists did not want to pay British taxes. They fought a war and won. They set up a new country: the United States of America (USA).

American Revolutionary War

In 1773 Americans protested about the tea tax by boarding British tea ships in Boston and throwing the tea into the harbour.

Soon war broke out. The Americans wrote a Declaration of Independence saying they now governed themselves.

End of the war

By 1781 the British knew they could not win. The USA became an independent country. Leading Americans wrote a constitution – a document that set out how the country would be run, and that gave its people rights.

The Americans' protests about the tea tax are known as the Boston Tea Party.

Key

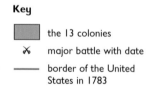
the 13 colonies

✗ major battle with date

— border of the United States in 1783

KEY DATES

1773 Boston Tea Party
1775 Fighting begins
1776 Declaration of Independence
1783 Peace of Paris ends the war
1789 George Washington becomes first US president

▽ Where the main battles were fought in the American Revolutionary War.

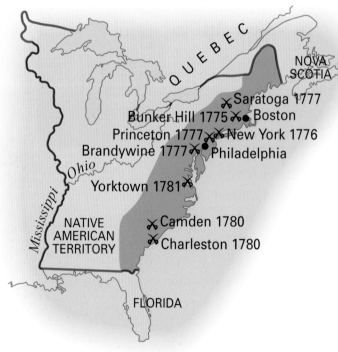

QUEBEC

NOVA SCOTIA

✗ Saratoga 1777

Bunker Hill 1775 ✗● Boston

Princeton 1777 ✗✗ New York 1776

Brandywine 1777 ✗● Philadelphia

Ohio

Yorktown 1781 ✗

Mississippi

NATIVE AMERICAN TERRITORY

✗ Camden 1780

✗ Charleston 1780

FLORIDA

French Revolution

During the French Revolution the people of France rose up against their rulers. They were fed up of having no say in how their country was run.

They set up a parliament, executed the king and spread their ideas of freedom and fairness across Europe and beyond.

Rising up

In 1789 the French rose up against King Louis XVI. They wanted liberty (freedom), equality and fraternity (brotherhood), and they set up a parliament.

But they also began executing people who they saw as their enemies. This time was known as the Terror.

The leader of the Terror, a man called Maximilien Robespierre, was beheaded in 1794. ▽▽

French people attacking the △△ Bastille prison in Paris.

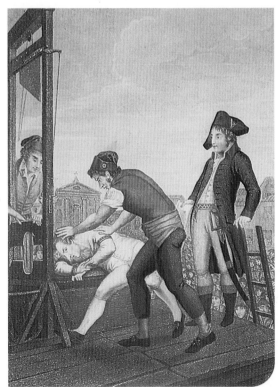

KEY DATES

1789 Revolution breaks out
1791 King Louis XVI under arrest
1793 Louis XVI beheaded; Terror begins
1794 Terror ends
1804 Napoleon makes himself emperor

Settling down

When the executions began, other nations invaded France to stop the Revolution spreading.

France hung on. Soon its most successful general, Napoleon Bonaparte, became emperor of much of western Europe.

World War I

World War I, from 1914 to 1918, was fought between the Allies (including Britain, France and Russia) and the Central Powers (including Germany and Austria-Hungary).

There was fighting around the world on land and sea and, for the first time, in the air. Some 10 million people lost their lives.

British soldiers leaving their trench to attack. △

▽ An early British tank.

Trench warfare

Machine guns were the main weapon. To shelter from bullets and shells, troops dug hundreds of kilometres of trenches. Neither side really advanced until the invention of tanks, around 1917.

Total war

Men had to join the armed forces and women had to work. Both sides tried to cut off their enemies' food supplies. German submarines torpedoed American boats carrying food to Britain, so in 1917 the USA joined the war. By the end of 1918, the Central Powers were defeated.

THESE WOMEN ARE DOING THEIR BIT

LEARN TO MAKE MUNITIONS

A poster encouraging △ women to work in the weapons factories.

Key

◻ Allies
◻ Central Powers
◻ neutral country

◁◁ Europe during World War I.

SWEDEN
North Sea
Baltic Sea
UNITED KINGDOM
GERMANY
BELGIUM
ATLANTIC OCEAN
FRANCE
SWITZ.
• Vienna
AUSTRIA-HUNGARY
RUSSIA
ITALY
Sarajevo •
MONTENEGRO
SERBIA
ROMANIA
BULGARIA
Black Sea
PORTUGAL
SPAIN
ALBANIA
GREECE
Gallipoli
OTTOMAN EMPIRE (TURKEY)
Mediterranean Sea
Cyprus

DID YOU KNOW?

People called World War I the 'war to end all wars' – but 20 years later, Europe was at war again.

World War II

More than 50 million people lost their lives in World War II (1939–1945), including many civilians.

During the war German Nazis carried out the Holocaust – they rounded up and killed people they did not like, especially the Jews. The war ended with more horror – the nuclear attack on Japan.

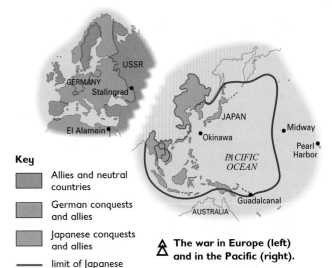

Key

- Allies and neutral countries
- German conquests and allies
- Japanese conquests and allies
- — limit of Japanese conquests

⚠ The war in Europe (left) and in the Pacific (right).

War begins

In 1937 Japan invaded China, the first step in its plan to take over South-east Asia. The German leader, Adolf Hitler, also wanted to build an empire. His invasion of Poland led to war in Europe.

Russians searching for relatives after the German attack on the city of Kursk, 1943. ⚠

KEY DATES

1937	Japan attacks China
1939	Germany invades Poland and war breaks out in Europe
1941	Japanese attack Pearl Harbor
1942	Germans besiege Stalingrad, Russia
1944	D-Day (6 June)
1945	Germany surrenders; atomic bombs on Japan

⚠ On D-Day Allied soldiers landed in northern France and began to push back the Germans.

Russia and America

In 1941 the war spread. Hitler's troops moved into Russia. Japan attacked an American base, Pearl Harbor, and the USA entered the war.

Over the next four years US troops pushed back the Japanese in Asia. Germany was retreating in Europe, too.

Last months

In May 1945 Germany surrendered (gave up). The Japanese had lost all their conquests. In August the USA dropped atomic bombs on two Japanese cities. Japan surrendered six days later.

Human rights

Most people agree that every human being should be able to rely on certain things, such as not being tortured or made a slave. These basic rights should be the same for everyone.

When rights are protected by law in a country, they are known as civil rights.

African slaves working on a sugar plantation in the Caribbean in the early 1800s. △

Human rights

Most of the countries in the United Nations have agreed to an International Bill of Human Rights. It lists many basic rights, including the right to life and the right to vote.

Different groups

One important right is that everyone should be equal in the eyes of the law. But people from certain groups are sometimes not treated fairly – perhaps because of their skin colour, sex or age.

△ Emmeline Pankhurst (1858–1928) being arrested. She campaigned for British women's right to vote.

Inside a US courtroom. In most countries people have the right to a fair trial. ▽

DID YOU KNOW?

The first country to give women the right to vote was New Zealand in 1893. In some countries women still do not have the vote.

◄◄ Archbishop Desmond Tuto fought against racism in his country, South Africa.

Abuse of power

Sometimes governments ignore human rights. Between 1948 and 1994 black people in South Africa were not allowed to vote, for example. Abuses of human rights are going on around the world right now.

Communism

Communism is the belief that society should be a commune – a place where everyone shares what they need to live.

Communists argue that societies where a few rich people own everything are unfair. But countries which tried to be communist in the 20th century were not fair either.

A poster of the Russian ▷▷ communist Vladimir Lenin (1870–1924), designed to show him as a hero.

Communism in Russia

The communist leader Vladimir Lenin won power in Russia in 1917, but died soon afterwards. The government took control of everything. People had to follow orders and work hard. Russians returned to capitalism in 1991.

Communism in China

In 1949 the communist leader Mao Zedong took control of China. After some terrible mistakes, China slowly turned back to capitalism at the end of the 20th century.

▽▽ Mao Zedong (1893-1976) used these Chinese teenagers, the Red Guards, to defend his ideas.

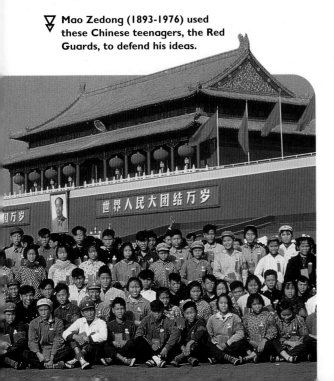

Karl Marx

The German thinker Karl Marx came up with the idea of modern communism. He urged poor workers to take over their countries and make them communist.

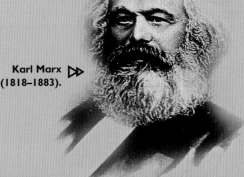

Karl Marx ▷▷
(1818–1883).

155

Map of the world

There are about 190 independent countries in the world, but the number changes. Sometimes countries split to form two or more new countries. Sometimes two countries join together.

To find a country on the map, look at the alphabetical list (right). After the country name is a grid reference to help you find it. There was not enough space on the map to label every country. The key (bottom right) tells you what any letters stand for.

List of countries

Afghanistan C13
Albania B10
Algeria C9–10
Andorra B10
Angola E10
Antigua & Barbuda D6
Argentina F6–G6
Armenia B12–C12
Australia F15–17
Austria B10
Azerbaijan B12–C12
Bahamas C6
Bahrain C12
Bangladesh C14
Barbados D7
Belarus B11
Belgium B10
Belize D5
Benin D10
Bhutan C14
Bolivia E6
Bosnia & Herzegovina B10
Botswana F11
Brazil E7–F7
Brunei Darussalam D15
Bulgaria B11
Burkina Faso D9
Burma (Myanmar) C14–D14

Burundi E11
Cambodia D15
Cameroon D10
Canada B3–7
Cape Verde D8
Central African Republic D10–11
Chad D10–11
Chile E6–G6
China C13–15
Colombia D6
Comoros E12
Congo D10–E10
Congo, Democratic Republic of D10–E11
Costa Rica D5
Côte d'Ivoire D9
Croatia B10
Cuba C5–6
Cyprus C11
Czech Republic B10
Denmark B10
Djibouti D12
Dominica D6
Dominican Republic D6
Ecuador E6
Egypt C11
Egypt C11
El Salvador D5

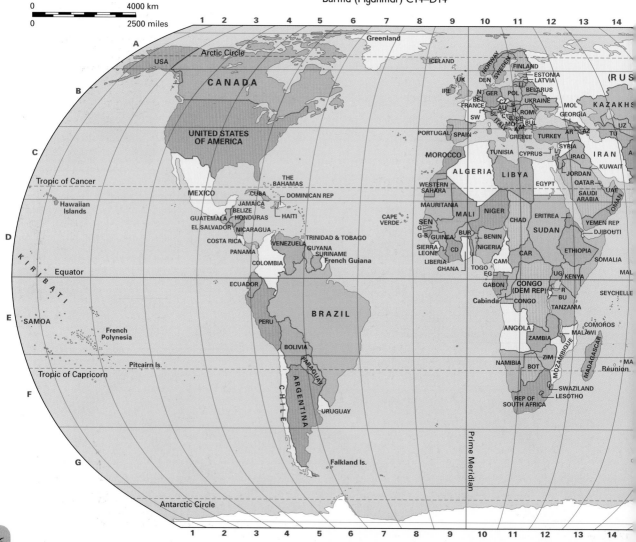

0 — 4000 km
0 — 2500 miles

Equatorial Guinea D10
Eritrea D11
Estonia B11
Ethiopia D11–12
Fiji E18
Finland A11
France B10
Gabon D10–E10
Gambia D9
Georgia B12
Germany B10
Ghana D9–10
Greece C11
Grenada D6
Guatemala D5
Guinea D9
Guinea-Bissau D9
Guyana D7
Haiti D6
Honduras D5
Hungary B10–11
Iceland A9
India C13–D13
Indonesia E15–17
Iran C12
Iraq C12
Ireland, Republic B9
Israel C11
Italy B10–C10

Jamaica D6
Japan C16–17
Jordan C11
Kazakhstan B12–13
Kenya D11–E11
Kirgyzstan B13
Kiribati D18–E18
Kuwait C12
Laos D15
Latvia B11
Lebanon C11
Lesotho F11
Liberia D9
Libya C10–11
Liechtenstein (see Europe
map, page 160)
Lithuania B11
Luxembourg B10
Macedonia B11
Madagascar E12–F12
Malawi E11
Malaysia D15
Maldives D13
Mali C9–D9
Malta C10
Mauritania C9–D9
Mauritius F12
Mexico C4–5
Moldova B11
Monaco B10
Mongolia B14–15
Montenegro B10
Morocco C9
Mozambique E11–F11
Namibia F10

Nauru E18
Nepal C14
Netherlands B10
New Zealand F18–G18
Nicaragua D5
Niger D10
Nigeria D10
North Korea B16–C16
Norway A10
Oman C12–D12
Pakistan C13
Palau D16
Panama D5–6
Papua New Guinea E17
Paraguay F7
Peru E6
Philippines D16
Poland B10–11
Portugal C9
Qatar C12
Romania B11
Russia B11–A19
Rwanda E11
St Kitts-Nevis D6
St Lucia D6
St Vincent
& the Grenadines D6
Samoa E1
San Marino
(see Europe map, page 160)
São Tomé & Principe D10
Saudi Arabia C12–D12
Senegal D9
Serbia B11
Seychelles E12
Sierra Leone D9
Singapore D15
Slovakia B10–11
Slovenia B10

Solomon Islands E18
Somalia D12
South Africa F11
South Korea C16
Spain B9–C9
Sri Lanka D14
Sudan D11
Suriname D7
Swaziland F11
Sweden A10–B10
Switzerland B10
Syria C11
Taiwan C16
Tajikistan C13
Tanzania E11
Thailand D14–15
Togo D10
Tonga E19–F19
Trinidad & Tobago D6
Tunisia C10
Turkey C11–12
Turkmenistan C12–13
Tuvalu E18
Uganda D11–E11
Ukraine B11
United Arab Emirates C12
United Kingdom B9
United States of America
B4–C4
Uruguay F7
Uzbekistan B13–C13
Vanuatu E18
Vatican City (see Europe
map, page 160)
Venezuela D6
Vietnam C15–D15
Yemen D12
Zambia E11
Zimbabwe E11–F11

Key			
A	ALBANIA	GER	GERMANY
AFG	AFGHANISTAN	H	HUNGARY
AR	ARMENIA	I	ISRAEL
AU	AUSTRIA	IRE	REPUBLIC OF
AZ	AZERBAIJAN		IRELAND
B	BOSNIA &	L	LEBANON
	HERZEGOVINA	LI	LITHUANIA
BE	BELGIUM	M	MACEDONIA
BD	BRUNEI	MO	MONTENEGRO
	DARUSSALAM	MOL	MOLDOVA
BOT	BOTSWANA	N	NETHERLANDS
BU	BURUNDI	POL	POLAND
BUL	BULGARIA	R	RWANDA
BUR	BURKINA FASO	ROM	ROMANIA
C	CROATIA	S	SLOVAKIA
CAM	CAMEROON	SE	SERBIA
CAR	CENTRAL	SEN	SENEGAL
	AFRICAN	SL	SLOVENIA
	REPUBLIC	SW	SWITZERLAND
CD	CÔTE D'IVOIRE	TU	TURKMENISTAN
CZ	CZECH	UAE	UNITED ARAB
	REPUBLIC		EMIRATES
DEN	DENMARK	UG	UGANDA
EG	EQUATORIAL	UK	UNITED
	GUINEA		KINGDOM
G	GAMBIA	UZ	UZBEKISTAN
G-B	GUINEA-BISSAU	ZIM	ZIMBABWE

Europe

Europe is the second smallest continent after Oceania. It is also the most crowded. It has about 45 countries.

Europe is separated from Asia by a chain of mountains called the Urals. Together the two continents form one massive supercontinent called Eurasia.

▽ Kiev is the capital of Ukraine. Like Russia, Ukraine is partly in Asia and partly in Europe.

▽ The busy Rhine River flows through central Europe.

▽ Norway is part of Scandinavia, the most northerly part of Europe.

Land and climate

Europe has many landscapes. There are wild mountainous areas in Scandinavia, the Alps and the Balkans. Rolling grasslands stretch from France to Russia.

◀◀ **Ireland, in the far west of Europe, faces the Atlantic Ocean.**

The area in the south around the Mediterranean has hot, dry summers and warm, wet winters. The far north lies in the cold Arctic region.

The European Union

In 1957 six European countries decided to work together more closely. They formed the European Economic Community, which later became the European Union (EU).

Thirty years later, the EU had 27 member countries. Over half had agreed to use the same currency (money), the euro.

The EU is run by a parliament, a council, and a commission that looks after laws and treaties.

The European Commission Building in Brussels, Belgium. ▷▷

Plant life

Europe used to be covered by trees. People cleared them for farmland thousands of years ago, but over one-quarter of Europe is still forest.

▽ **Pines and scrubby bushes grow along the Mediterranean coast.**

Animals

Larger European animals include the brown bear, wolf, red fox and types of deer. Birds range from wrens to owls and hawks. There are many kinds of insect, mollusc, fish and frog.

Way of life

Most European people live in cities. Many live comfortably because their countries are rich from industry, farming and natural resources.

Europe has a mix of cultures. It is known for its classical music and long tradition of fine painting. The main religion is Christianity.

FAST FACTS ▶▶

Largest country:	Russia (17,075,400 sq km)
Smallest country:	Vatican City (0.44 sq km)
Tallest mountain:	Elbrus, Russia (5642 m)
Longest river:	Volga, Russia (3690 km)
Largest freshwater lake:	Ladoga, Russia (17,700 sq km)

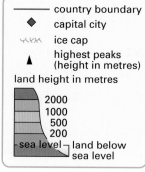

— country boundary
◆ capital city
ᴋᴋᴋ ice cap
▲ highest peaks (height in metres)
land height in metres
2000
1000
500
200
sea level — land below sea level

LUX   LUXEMBOURG
LIE   LIECHTENSTEIN
NETH   NETHERLANDS

France

France is the largest country in western Europe. It has many different landscapes and ways of life.

France is famous for its fine wines and for its cheeses, such as Brie and Camembert. French cooking is enjoyed around the world.

Food and farming

French crops include wheat, maize (corn) and sunflowers, which provide food for animals and oil for cooking. Some farmers grow grapes to make wine.

The Eiffel Tower is a famous landmark in France's capital city, Paris.

Industry

France's biggest industry is tourism. The country also makes cars, high-speed trains and Ariane space rockets. Most electricity comes from nuclear power stations or hydroelectric dams (where energy from rushing water is turned into electricity).

French wines are made from grapes that grow in vineyards like this one.

History

The name 'France' comes from the tribe of Franks who invaded in the AD 400s. Before then, France was a Roman province. France was ruled by kings from the time of the Franks until 1789, when there was a revolution (see page 151). Since then, it has been a republic.

(see page 151)

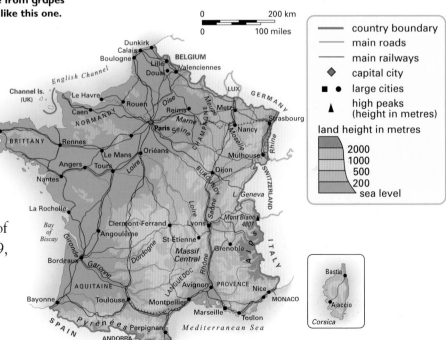

0	200 km
0	100 miles

country boundary
main roads
main railways
◆ capital city
■ ● large cities
▲ high peaks (height in metres)
land height in metres
2000
1000
500
200
sea level

Germany

Germany is a large country in the middle of Europe. It is one of the world's richest countries, and it is a strong member of the European Union.

Germany is famous for its electrical equipment and cars.

Land and farming

Northern Germany has low hills and flat plains. To the south are the Black Forest and the snowy Alps. The climate is mild. German farmers grow wheat, maize (corn), potatoes and grapes.

The city of Frankfurt is home to 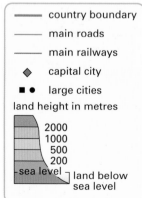 the European Central Bank.

Germany was split for 40 years. In 1989, the wall between East and West Berlin came down at last.

Industry

German factories produce machine tools, electrical goods, chemicals and cars. Most Germans work in factories or in service industries such as banks and hotels.

Ruling the country

Germany is divided into 16 states, each with its own parliament and local laws. Each state sends representatives to the national parliament in Berlin.

0   200 km
0   100 miles

DENMARK
Baltic Sea
North Sea
Hamburg
Bremen
Ems
Weser
Elbe
Hannover   Berlin
NETHERLANDS
POLAND
SAXONY
Duisburg   Essen
Düsseldorf   Dortmund   Leipzig
RUHR
Cologne
Bonn
BELGIUM
Frankfurt
Mosel
Main
CZECH REPUBLIC
LUX
Rhine
Nuremberg
FRANCE
Black Forest
Stuttgart
BAVARIA
Danube
Munich
L. Constance
Alps
SWITZERLAND   AUSTRIA

——— country boundary
——— main roads
——— main railways
◆ capital city
■ ● large cities
land height in metres

2000
1000
500
200
sea level   land below sea level

Russia

Russia is the largest country in the world – almost as big as the USA and Canada put together. It stretches across two continents, Europe and Asia.

Russia is famous for being the first country to put a person in space.

This monument in ▷▷ the capital, Moscow, celebrates space exploration.

⚠ In the far north, some people live as reindeer herders.

The land

The European and Asian parts of Russia are separated by the low Ural Mountains. To the east is a bleak, forested area called Siberia. To the far north is tundra (frozen land).

Making a living

Russia produces timber (wood) from its vast forests. It mines oil, natural gas, coal and useful metals such as copper, iron ore, gold and silver.

Ruling Russia

Early rulers of Russia were called tsars (emperors). In 1917 there was a revolution. Russia became a communist state known as the Soviet Union. In 1991, the union fell apart. Russians voted for the first time.

DID YOU KNOW?

Russia is around 8000 km wide. It's so big that when it is morning in west of the country, it is already evening in the far east!

---

country boundary
main roads
main railways
◆ capital city
■ ● large cities

land height in metres

2000
1000
500
200
sea level ⌐ land below sea level

0 ——— 500 km
0 ——— 250 miles

FAST FACTS ▷▷

Capital city: *Moscow*
Population: *143,025,000*
Area: *17,075,400 sq km*
Language: *Russian*
Religion: *Christian*
Currency: *1 rouble = 100 kopecks*
Wealth per person: *$9620*

Italy

Italy has spectacular cities, fine art, beautiful buildings and delicious food.

It is a boot-shaped strip of land that sticks out into the Mediterranean Sea. It has a warm, sunny climate.

North and south

Factories in the north of Italy make cars, clothes and shoes. The richest farmland is also in the north. Italian farmers grow wheat, sugar beet, rice, vegetables and fruit, including grapes for wine.

△ Florence Cathedral is famous for its great dome, built in 1436.

△ The north-eastern city of Venice is built on islands in a lagoon.

FAST FACTS ▷▷

Capital city: Rome
Population: 58,742,000
Area: 301,270 sq km
Language: Italian
Religion: Christian
Currency: 1 euro = 100 cents
Wealth per person: $27,860

▽ The Grand Duke's Madonna (1505) by the Renaissance artist Raphael.

From empire to nation

The powerful Roman empire grew up around the Italian city of Rome. It collapsed around AD 400.

From the Middle Ages Italy was made up of small city states, including Venice, Florence and Naples. Between 1350 and 1550 these states were at the heart of a flowering of culture known as the Renaissance. Italy became a single country in the 1860s.

Spain

Spain is a large, mountainous country in southern Europe. The north is wet, but central and southern Spain is dry.

The country has an exciting history. Today it is Roman Catholic – but for nearly 500 years most of Spain was an Islamic country.

The Mediterranean port of Barcelona is Spain's second largest city.

A small, traditional farm in the Spanish countryside.

Fish and other business

Spain has more fishing trawlers than any other country in Europe. Most of its fishing grounds are in the Atlantic Ocean.

Spanish farmers grow oranges, olives, wheat and barley.

Northern Spain has factories that make cars, books and electrical goods. Southern and eastern Spain has a busy tourist industry.

FAST FACTS

Capital city: Madrid
Population: 43,484,000
Area: 505,990 sq km
Language: Spanish, Catalan, Galician, Basque
Religion: Christian
Currency: 1 euro = 100 cents
Wealth per person: $25,070

Spanish history

Between around 710 and 1200 Spain was ruled by Muslims called Moors. Christian kingdoms in the north gradually reconquered the country. In the 1500s Spain built up an empire in Central and South America.

There was a civil war in Spain in the 1930s. Since the 1970s, Spain has had a king again, but the country is ruled by a government elected by the people.

The Moors built beautiful buildings, such as this mosque in the city of Granada.

United Kingdom

The United Kingdom (UK) is made up of England, Scotland, Wales and Northern Ireland. Scotland has its own parliament. Wales and Northern Ireland have national assemblies.

The UK is small, but it once ruled a large empire. The English language is still spoken in many parts of the world.

The UK Parliament meets in this grand building, on the banks of the River Thames in London.

Snowdonia in north Wales is an area of beautiful mountain scenery.

Land and sea

British farmers raise cattle and sheep. The main crops are wheat, barley, oats, potatoes and sugar beet. British boats fish in the Atlantic and North Sea.

British industry

UK cities were home to the world's first modern factories. Today the United Kingdom makes cars, chemicals and other products. It is a centre of banking, publishing and tourism.

British people

Over its history, many peoples settled in Britain, including Romans, Anglo-Saxons, Vikings and Normans. Today the UK is home to a mix of cultures, with strong Caribbean and southern Asian communities.

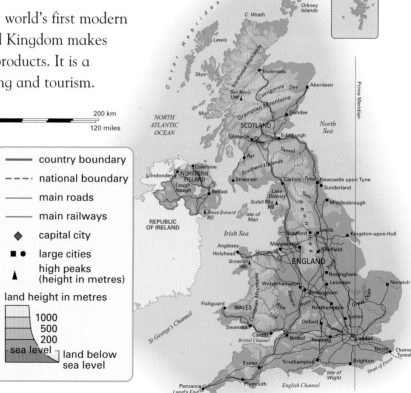

	200 km
0	
0	120 miles

country boundary
national boundary
main roads
main railways
◆ capital city
■ ● large cities
▲ high peaks (height in metres)

land height in metres

1000
500
200
sea level — land below sea level

Asia

Asia is the largest continent in the world. It covers one-third of the Earth's land surface and contains more than 45 countries.

Asia has some of the world's busiest cities. More people live in Asia than any other continent.

- country boundary
- ice cap
- ▲ highest peaks (height in metres)
- land height in metres

| 5000 |
| 2000 |
| 1000 |
| 500 |
| 200 |
| sea level — land below sea level |

0   1000 km
0   500 miles

AR	ARMENIA
AZ	AZERBAIJAN
BH	BHUTAN
BR	BRUNEI
GE	GEORGIA
IS	ISRAEL
JO	JORDAN
LE	LEBANON
NK	NORTH KOREA
SK	SOUTH KOREA
TU	TURKMENISTAN
UAE	UNITED ARAB EMIRATES

Land and climate

Asia has flat, frozen plains in the far north, then a band of coniferous forest. Central Asia is mostly grassland or desert.

South and South-east Asia are separated from the rest of the continent by the Himalayas – the world's tallest mountains. The south has a hot, wet climate with some tropical rainforests.

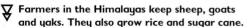
Farmers in the Himalayas keep sheep, goats and yaks. They also grow rice and sugar cane.

Animals

Many beautiful plants first came from Asia, including tulips and rhododendrons.

Asia is home to amazing animals such as camels, tigers, pythons and giant pandas. Birds include peacocks and cranes. Colourful butterflies and beetles live in the tropical forests.

Orang-utans live on the islands of Borneo and Sumatra.

Oil

The Middle East, in western Asia, is mostly desert. Its countries have grown rich from oil wells in the desert and in an area of sea called the Persian Gulf. Many central Asian countries have oil, too, including Kazakhstan and Azerbaijan.

An oil refinery in Saudi Arabia. ▷▷

People

Asia has some of the world's poorest countries and some of its richest.

Most Asians live in the country and make their living from farming. On the coasts, people fish.

In the south more people are moving to cities. The two cities with the most people are Tokyo (Japan) and Bombay (India).

△ A fishing boat off the coast of Thailand.

▽ A rice farmer in Vietnam. Rice is the main crop in most of India, China and South-east Asia.

FAST FACTS ▷▷

Largest country:	China (9,572,900 sq km)
Smallest country:	Maldives (300 sq km)
Tallest mountain:	Everest, Nepal-China (8848 m)
Longest river:	Chiang Jiang (Yangtze), China (6380 km)
Largest freshwater lake:	Baykal, Russia (31,494 sq km)

▽ Angkor Wat is a group of Hindu temples in the Cambodian rainforest, built about 1000 years ago.

△ Many Asian cities are overcrowded. More than 10 million people live in Seoul, South Korea.

Culture

The first civilizations appeared in Asia. All the world's main religions began in Asia, too. Hinduism, Buddhism and Sikhism started in southern Asia. Judaism, Christianity and Islam started in the Middle East.

India and Pakistan

The two largest countries in South Asia are India and Pakistan. They were a single country until 1947. Now they are great rivals.

India has over a billion people. By 2030 it will have a bigger population than China.

India

Pakistan

Countryside

The Himalayas to the north contain the world's 20 highest peaks. The Indus, Ganges and Brahmaputra rivers flow down from these mountains.

Most people live by farming. In the north they grow wheat, lentils and cotton. In the hot, wet south, crops include rice and tropical fruits.

City life

Some people look for work in the big cities. Factories produce ships, bicycles, sewing machines and clothing. India has important computer, film and space industries.

History

South Asia's earliest civilization grew up in the Indus Valley around 2500 BC. Muslim emperors, the Mughals, ruled the region from 1526 to 1857, when it became part of the British Empire. In 1947 India and Pakistan became independent countries.

A coach in the mountains of northern Pakistan. Drivers decorate their buses and trucks.

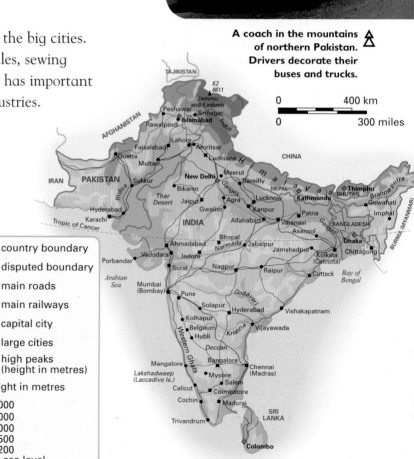

country boundary
disputed boundary
main roads
main railways
capital city
large cities
high peaks (height in metres)

land height in metres
5000
2000
1000
500
200
sea level

China

China has the world's biggest population. For almost 4000 years it was ruled by emperors. Since 1949 it has been led by the Chinese Communist Party.

China has a long history and rich culture. It is famous for its painting, silkwork and porcelain.

△ The craggy Huang Shan Mountains are in Anhui province, eastern China.

The land

Western China has deserts, grasslands and mountains. Bamboo forests cover central China. Southern China is hot and humid.

Two great rivers cross China from west to east – the Huang He (Yellow River) and the Chang Jiang (Yangtze).

Chinese people

Most of China's people are Han Chinese. They all write in the same language but have different spoken languages.

Making a living

Most people live in eastern and south-eastern China. Many work the land. In the north they grow wheat and potatoes. In the south they grow rice.

China's cities are getting bigger. Chinese factories make nearly three-quarters of the world's toys. They also produce steel, textiles, shoes, ships and cars.

▽ The Great Wall of China is over 6000 km long.

DID YOU KNOW?

Many great inventions originally came from China. They include the compass, paper money, steel and fireworks!

▽ Bicycles are the most important transport in China.

Early China

Chinese civilization is very old. Qin Shi Huangdi, the first emperor of the Qin dynasty (family), made China a single country in 221 BC. He built the Great Wall to keep out enemy tribes.

Mongols and Ming

In the 1200s the Mongols (people from central Asia) conquered China. They were defeated in 1368 by the Ming dynasty. Ming emperors built the Forbidden City, a great palace in Beijing.

The communist leader Mao Zedong ruled China from 1949 until 1976.

Troubled times

In 1911 the Chinese emperor was overthrown. There was unrest and in 1945 civil war broke out. The communists won and set up the People's Republic of China. The state took over all farming and industry.

Chinese religions

China's two great religions, Taoism and Confucianism, are based on teachings from around 500 BC. Laozi, founder of Taoism, said people should try to live in harmony with nature. Confucius (Kongzi) said that everyone in society should know their place. Buddhism reached China from India around AD 60. Under the communists, religion was banned for a time.

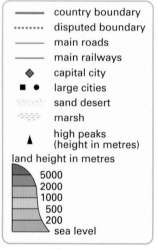

The Chinese thinker Confucius (551–479 BC).

China's growth

Since the 1980s, private businesses have started up, but the government still controls many parts of Chinese life. In 1997 Hong Kong became part of China.

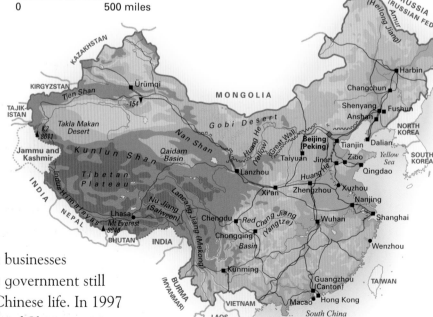

Map legend:
- country boundary
- disputed boundary
- main roads
- main railways
- capital city
- large cities
- sand desert
- marsh
- high peaks (height in metres)

land height in metres
- 5000
- 2000
- 1000
- 500
- 200
- sea level

0   800 km
0   500 miles

Japan

Japan is a string of islands off eastern Asia. It is one of the world's wealthiest countries. Its electronic goods sell all over the world.

Japan is also famous for its delicious food, beautiful gardens and martial arts.

━━	country boundary
━━	main roads
━━	main railways
◆	capital city
■●	large cities
▲	high peaks (height in metres)

land height in metres
2000
1000
500
200
sea level

0   400 km
0   200 miles

RUSSIA
Sea of Okhotsk
Hokkaido
Sapporo
PACIFIC OCEAN
Tsugaru Channel
Sea of Japan
Sendai
Sado
Honshu
Mt Fuji 3776 ▲   Tokyo
Yokohama
Oki Is.
Kyoto
Nagoya
Izu Is.
Kobe Osaka
Hiroshima
Kitakyushu
Fukuoka
Shikoku
PACIFIC OCEAN
Kyushu
East China Sea
Kagoshima
Osumi Is. (Ryukyu Is.)

This view of Mount Fuji was painted by the artist Hokusai (1760–1849).

Mountains and volcanoes

Two-thirds of Japan is wooded mountains. The tallest mountain, Mount Fuji, is an old volcano. Japan has more than 60 active volcanoes and is often shaken by earthquakes.

Working

Japan has one of the world's biggest fishing fleets. Boats bring back tonnes of fish each morning. Japanese farmers grow rice.

Japan is an important producer of cars, ships, television sets and electronic equipment.

Tokyo, the Japanese capital, is one of the world's largest, most modern cities.

The empire

Japan has been ruled by an emperor since the 500s BC. Between 1160 until 1867 lords called shoguns ruled in the name of the emperor. Today Japan is run by a parliament and the emperor has no real power.

A samurai warrior. A samurai was a knight who served a shogun.

North America

North America stretches from Canada in the north to the Caribbean in the south. It contains more than 20 countries.

Mountains run down the sides of North America, with huge plains in between. There are deserts in the south-west.

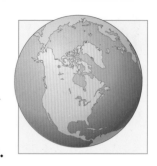

Animals and plants

North America has redwoods (the world's tallest trees) and bristlecone pines (the oldest trees). It is home to brown bears, raccoons and skunks.

The deserts contain cacti, rattlesnakes and tarantulas. The southern rainforests have toucans and other colourful birds.

◀◀ An Alaskan brown bear fishes for salmon.

FAST FACTS

Largest country:	Canada (9,970,645 sq km)
Smallest country:	El Salvador (21,040 sq km)
Tallest mountain:	McKinley (Denali), Alaska (6194 m)
Longest river:	Mississippi-Missouri, USA (6270 km)
Largest freshwater lake:	Lake Superior, USA (83,270 sq km)

◀◀ A Native American totem pole from Vancouver, on Canada's west coast.

Coming to North America

The first settlers arrived in North America about 15,000 years ago from Asia. They lived by hunting, fishing and farming. European settlers arrived 500 years ago.

ARCTIC OCEAN

ASIA

USA
Mt. McKinley 6194
Beaufort Sea
Queen Elizabeth Islands
Greenland (Denmark)
Arctic Circle

Mt. Logan 5951
Mackenzie
Victoria Island
Baffin Bay
Baffin Island
Davis Strait

PACIFIC OCEAN

ROCKY MOUNTAINS

Great Bear L.

Peace

Great Slave L.

Vancouver
Seattle
Edmonton
Calgary

CANADA

Hudson Bay

Lake Winnipeg
Winnipeg

Prairies

San Francisco
SIERRA NEVADA
Snake
Death Valley
Los Angeles
Colorado
Grand Canyon

Great Plains
Missouri

The Great Lakes
Chicago
Detroit
Toronto
Ottawa
Montreal
St Lawrence
Boston
New York

Newfoundland

St Pierre & Miquelon (France)

UNITED STATES OF AMERICA
Ohio
Mississippi
APPALACHIANS
Philadelphia
Washington D.C.
Atlanta

ATLANTIC OCEAN

SIERRA MADRE
Rio Grande
Houston

Monterrey
Gulf of Mexico

PACIFIC OCEAN

MEXICO
Guadalajara
Mexico City
5452
Popocatepetl
Yucatan Peninsula
CUBA
THE BAHAMAS
Tropic of Cancer
Puerto Rico (USA)
DOMINICAN REPUBLIC
JAMAICA
HAITI
ST KITTS & NEVIS
ANTIGUA & BARBUDA
ST LUCIA
DOMINICA
Belmopan
BELIZE
GUATEMALA
HONDURAS
Guatemala City
Tegucigalpa
San Salvador
EL SALVADOR
NICARAGUA
Managua
San José
COSTA RICA
Caribbean Sea
Panama Canal
Panama City
PANAMA
ST VINCENT & THE GRENADINES
BARBADOS
GRENADA
TRINIDAD & TOBAGO
SOUTH AMERICA

0 — 1000 km
0 — 500 miles

⎯⎯	country boundary	land height in metres
◆	capital city	2000
■	large city	1000
⋎⋋⋎	ice cap	500
▲	highest peaks (height in metres)	200
		sea level ⌐ land below sea level

Canada

Canada is the second biggest country in the world, but much of it is almost empty of people.

The north is a wasteland of snow and ice. The Rocky Mountains lie in the west and wide grasslands (prairies) stretch across the centre.

Cold climate

Snow covers much of Canada from November to April. Over half of the country is forested. Farmers grow wheat on the prairies.

▽ Most French-speaking Canadians live in Québec. The province's capital is Québec City.

△ Peyto Lake in Canada's Rocky Mountains.

FAST FACTS

Capital city: Ottawa
Population: 32,225,000
Area: 9,970,645 sq km
Language: English, French
Religion: Christian
Currency: 1 Canadian dollar = 100 cents
Wealth per person: $30,66

◁◁ Clearing snowy roads in Ottawa, the Canadian capital.

People

Many Canadians trace their families to French and British settlers who arrived nearly 500 years ago.

About 500,000 Native Americans live in Canada. They include the Inuit of the far north, the Haida of the west coast and the Cree.

Wealth

Canada is one of the world's richest countries. It has timber, zinc, gold and other resources. Its factories produce telecommunications equipment, machinery and cars.

United States of America

The United States of America (USA) is the world's richest and most powerful country. It has a large, well-equipped army.

American products sell around the world, and Hollywood films have spread the American way of life to many countries.

American film stars are famous all over the world. They include Marilyn Monroe, Will Smith – and Mickey Mouse!

⚠ The Grand Canyon is 446 km long and over 1.6 km deep. The Colorado River carved it out of the surrounding rock over thousands of years.

Land and climate

The USA is huge and has many different climates. Alaska is cold, while Florida is tropical. The south-west is dry, but the north-west is rainy.

The west coast has earthquakes. There are mountain ranges, such as the Rockies.

Central USA has grassy plains, where farmers grow wheat and raise cattle. The Mississippi and Missouri rivers drain the land.

People and cities

The USA has the third largest population of any country – nearly 300 million people. Most live in cities along the east or west coasts.

KEY DATES

1776	Britain's North American colonies declare their independence
1803	USA buys most of midwest America from France
1861	American Civil War begins
1865	American Civil War ends
1917	USA enters World War I
1941	USA enters World War II
1969	Americans land on the Moon

FAST FACTS

Capital city: Washington DC
Population: 296,483,000
Area: 9,629,090 sq km
Language: English, Spanish
Religion: Christian
Currency: 1 US dollar = 100 cents
Wealth per person: $39,710

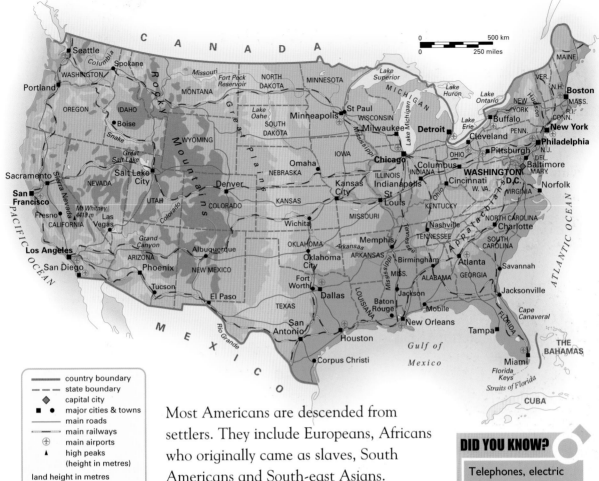

Map legend:

- country boundary
- state boundary
- ◆ capital city
- ■ ● major cities & towns
- main roads
- main railways
- ⊕ main airports
- ▲ high peaks (height in metres)

land height in metres
- 2000–5000
- 1000–2000
- 500–1000
- 200–500
- less than 200
- sea level — land below sea level

Most Americans are descended from settlers. They include Europeans, Africans who originally came as slaves, South Americans and South-east Asians.

Farms, mines and factories

American farmers produce wheat, potatoes, sugar beets, oranges, beef, cotton and tobacco. The country has lots of oil and gas, iron and copper, and salt. Factories make clothing, food, cars and computers.

Birth of a nation

The USA was born on 4 July 1776, when 13 British colonies became an independent country (see page 150). The original USA was small, but it bought or seized more land. The Native Americans lost most of their land.

DID YOU KNOW?

Telephones, electric lights, aeroplanes, nuclear weapons and the silicon chip were all invented in the USA.

▽ Sitting Bull, a chief of the Sioux people, won a great victory at the Battle of Little Bighorn (1876). ▽

▽ The Statue of Liberty stands in New York Harbour. Her torch represents freedom.

177

Caribbean

The Caribbean is a group of tropical islands scattered across the Caribbean Sea, between North and South America.

During the rainy season, these islands are sometimes hit by enormous storms called hurricanes.

Working life

Many Caribbean people work on large farms called plantations. They grow sugar cane, bananas, coffee, spices and other tropical crops. The Caribbean has many tourist visitors.

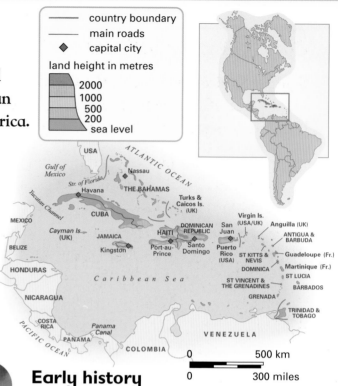

⚠ Barbados and other Caribbean islands are famous for their long sandy beaches and warm seas.

Slavery and freedom

European settlers brought West Africans to the Caribbean to work as slaves on plantations. Slavery ended in 1886 but conditions for black people remained poor.

During the 20th century most Caribbean countries gained independence from the Spanish.

DID YOU KNOW?

There are more than 20 countries in the Caribbean.

Early history

Five hundred years ago the Caribbean islands were home to two groups of Native Americans, the Arawaks and the Caribs.

In the 1500s the Spanish conquered the Caribbean. Later French, Dutch and English sailors captured some islands.

Cuba

Cuba is the largest Caribbean island and home to more than 11 million people. It gained independence in 1898. Cuba became a communist country in 1959, under the leadership of Fidel Castro. The country is famous for its rich music and fine cigars.

◀◀ Fidel Castro.

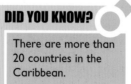

South America

South America has some of the world's largest cities – and some of the wildest, remotest places you could imagine. It is made up of 13 countries.

South America's rainforests and mountains contain amazing wildlife, but much of it is under threat as land is cleared for mines, ranches or farms.

△ More than 10 million people live in the Brazilian city of Rio de Janeiro. Most live in shacks called favelas.

FAST FACTS

Largest country:	Brazil (8,547,400 sq km)
Smallest country:	Suriname (163,270 sq km)
Tallest mountain:	Aconcagua, Argentina (6960 m)
Longest river:	Amazon (6452 km)
Largest freshwater lake:	Titicaca, Peru (8290 sq km)

The Iguacu Falls, on the border between Brazil and ▽ Argentina, are made up of nearly 300 waterfalls.

Wet or dry

Rainforest covers most of the northern half of South America. The world's second longest river, the Amazon, flows through it.

The continent is also home to the driest place on Earth, the Atacama Desert.

Mountains, grass and ice

South America has the world's longest mountain range. The Andes stretch for 7242 kilometres down the western edge of the continent.

In the south there are grasslands called pampas. Farmers graze cattle here. The southern tip of the continent has glaciers.

▽ The village of Maras in the Peruvian Andes.

⚠ A destroyed area of Amazon rainforest.

Animals and plants

The rainforest is home to jaguars, sloths, parrots and monkeys. Piranhas swim in the River Amazon. The Andes has alpacas, vicunas and llamas, all relatives of the camel. There are penguins and seals in the far south.

▽ The Magellanic penguin breeds on the coasts of Argentina, Chile and the Falkland Islands.

People and history

The Native Americans of the Andes, such as the Nazcas, Chimus and Incas, developed great empires. But they could not stop the European invaders who arrived after 1492.

Portugal ruled Brazil, and brought in millions of African slaves to work on sugar, cotton and tobacco plantations (farms). Most of the rest of the continent belonged to Spain. The Spanish made the Native Americans work in their silver mines.

▽ The Aymará Indians of Bolivia still speak Quechua, the language of the Incas.

Independence

In the 1800s two South American generals led the fight for independence. José de San Martín won freedom for Argentina, Chile and Peru. Simón Bolívar won freedom for Bolivia, Colombia, Ecuador and Venezuela.

▽ Simón Bolívar.

country boundary
capital city
large city
highest peaks
(height in metres)

land height in metres
5000
2000
1000
500
200
sea level

Caribbean Sea

Barranquilla
Valencia
Maracaibo
Caracas
VENEZUELA
Georgetown
Paramaribo
Cayenne
French Guiana
(France)
Medellín
Orinoco
GUIANA HIGHLANDS
GUYANA
SURINAME
Bogotá
Cali
COLOMBIA

Equator

Quito
Cotopaxi
5896
Chimborazo
6310
ECUADOR
Guayaquil

Negro
Amazon
Manaus
Belem
Fortaleza

Madeira
Tapajos
Xingu
Tocantins
BRAZIL
São Francisco
Recife

A N D E S
PERU
Lima

Mato Grosso
Brasília
BRAZILIAN HIGHLANDS
Salvador

L. Titicaca
La Paz
BOLIVIA
Paraguay
Belo Horizonte
Paraná
BRAZIL PLATEAU

PACIFIC OCEAN

Atacama Desert
PARAGUAY
São Paulo
Rio de Janeiro
Nova Iguaçu

Tropic of Capricorn

Gran Chaco
Asunción
Curitiba

O C E A N
A T L A N T I C

Acongagua
6960
Córdoba
Rosario
URUGUAY
Pôrto Alegre

Santiago
Buenos Aires
Montevideo
Río de la Plata
C H I L E
A R G E N T I N A
Pampas

Patagonia

Falkland Islands (UK)

Tierra del Fuego

Cape Horn

0   1000 km
0   500 miles

South America now

Today's South Americans are a mix of Europeans, Africans and Native Americans. French Guiana is the only European colony.

South America has oil wells and precious minerals. It supplies the world with copper, tin, zinc, coffee, cocoa and fruit. Even so, most of the people remain terribly poor.

Africa

Africa is the world's second largest continent. It covers about one-fifth of the land on Earth.

Africa contains more than 50 countries, each with many different languages and peoples. Just 60 years ago, most of these countries were ruled by European nations.

EUROPE

Mediterranean Sea

ASIA

0 — 1000 km
0 — 500 miles

Rabat
Algiers
Casablanca
Canary Is.
(Spain)
MOROCCO
ATLAS MOUNTAINS
Tunis
TUNISIA
Tripoli
Alexandria
Cairo
Suez Canal

NORTH
ATLANTIC
OCEAN
WESTERN
SAHARA
ALGERIA
Sahara Desert
LIBYA
EGYPT
L. Nasser
Red Sea
Tropic of Cancer

CAPE
VERDE
MAURITANIA
Nouakchott
MALI
Niger
NIGER
CHAD
Khartoum
ERITREA
Asmara

SENEGAL
Dakar
THE GAMBIA
GUINEA-
BISSAU
Bissau
Bamako
BURKINA
Niamey
L. Chad
SUDAN
Djibouti DJIBOUTI
ETHIOPIA

Conakry
GUINEA
Freetown
BE
Ouagadougou
NIGERIA
Ndjamena
Addis Ababa

SIERRA LEONE
Monrovia
LIBERIA
CÔTE
D'IVOIRE
GHANA
T
Porto
Novo
Abuja
Lagos
CENTRAL
AFRICAN REPUBLIC
ETHIOPIAN
HIGHLANDS
SOMALIA

Yamoussoukro
Accra
CAMEROON
Mogadishu

EQUATORIAL GUINEA
SÃO TOMÉ &
PRINCIPE
Yaoundé
Bangui
UGANDA
KENYA
Equator

Libreville
GABON
CONGO
Congo
CONGO
(DEM. REP.)
Kampala
L. Victoria
RW
Kigali
BU
5895
Nairobi
Mt Kilimanjaro
INDIAN

Brazzaville
Cabinda
(Angola)
Kinshasa
Bujumbura
TANZANIA
Dodoma
Dar es Salaam
OCEAN
SEYCHELLES

SOUTH
ATLANTIC
OCEAN
Luanda
L. Tanganyika
L. Nyasa
(L. Malawi)
COMOROS

ANGOLA
ZAMBIA
Lusaka
Zambezi
MALAWI
Lilongwe
Mozambique Channel
Antananarivo
MAURITIUS

Harare
ZIMBABWE
MADAGASCAR
Tropic of Capricorn

BE BENIN
BU BURUNDI
RW RWANDA
T TOGO

NAMIBIA
Windhoek
BOTSWANA
Kalahari
Desert
Gaborone
Pretoria
Maputo
MOZAMBIQUE

Namib Desert
Johannesburg
SWAZILAND

REP. OF
SOUTH
AFRICA
Drakensberg
LESOTHO

Cape Town
Cape of
Good Hope

— country boundary
◆ capital city
■ large city
▲ highest peaks
(height in metres)
land height in metres
2000
1000
500
200
sea level — land below
sea level

⚠ At the Victoria Falls, between Zambia and Zimbabwe, the Zambezi River drops over a 100-m cliff.

The land

Nearly all of Africa is hot. There is tropical rainforest in the middle of the continent and savannah (grassland) to the south.

Africa has the world's largest hot desert, the Sahara, and the world's biggest river, the Nile.

People cross the Sahara, in north Africa, by camel. ▽

Animals

The savannah is home to lions, zebras, giraffes and elephants. Crocodiles, hippos and flamingos live in African wetlands. Monkeys, chimpanzees and gorillas live in the rainforests.

▽ A giraffe at a waterhole.

People and places

Africa does not have many big cities or factories. Most Africans live in villages. They keep a few animals and grow enough food for their family. Larger farms produce coffee, tea and peanuts (groundnuts) to sell abroad.

▽ Cape Town, South Africa, is one of Africa's most beautiful cities.

Moving around

Some African peoples live partly as nomads, moving around with their animals. The Bedouin of the Sahara and Masai of eastern Africa do this. A few, such as the Efe and the San, live by hunting animals and gathering wild foods. **Masai people.** ▶▶

The ancient Egyptian civilization grew up by the Nile around 4000 BC.

African history

Scientists believe that the first humans lived in Africa.

From the AD 400s, empires in West Africa used camels to carry gold, salt and slaves across the Sahara. Great Zimbabwe in the south was a centre of the gold trade.

From the 1500s Europeans took millions of African slaves and went on to control most of Africa. Since 1956 African states have won their independence.

The ruins of the ancient city of Great Zimbabwe.

Africa today

Much of Africa is very poor. Lack of rain in some countries has led to food shortages, hunger and disease. In other countries wars have caused much hardship.

Famines happen when crops fail. This Somalian boy is at a relief centre.

Oceania

Oceania is the smallest continent. It is made up of Australia, New Guinea, New Zealand and thousands of small Pacific islands.

The islands are split into three groups: Melanesia, Micronesia and Polynesia. Many have no people.

Landscapes

The Pacific islands are tropical, with mountains and rainforests. North-eastern Australia has rainforest, too. Off the coast lies the world's largest coral reef, the Great Barrier Reef.

The hot, dry area in the middle of Australia is known as the 'outback'. Much of it is desert.

New Zealand is split into two islands. North Island has forests, volcanoes and hot springs. South Island has mountains and glaciers.

Milford Sound on New Zealand's South Island is a fjord – a steep-sided valley flooded by the sea.

> **DID YOU KNOW?**
>
> Oceania is home to more than 30 million people. Nearly 6 million live in Papua New Guinea – and between them they speak more than 700 different languages!

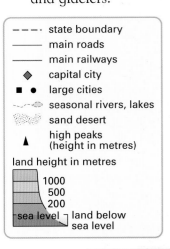

- – – – – state boundary
- ——— main roads
- ——— main railways
- ◆ capital city
- ■ ● large cities
- ∿∿ seasonal rivers, lakes
- sand desert
- ▲ high peaks (height in metres)

land height in metres

1000
500
200
sea level · land below sea level

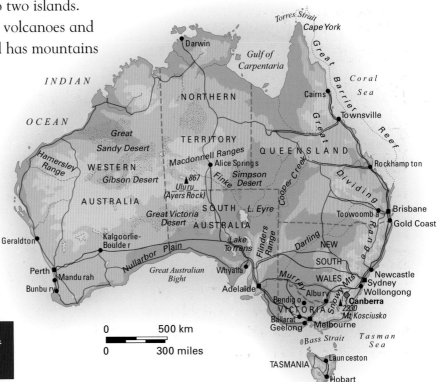

Animals and plants

Many Australian animals and plants live nowhere else on Earth. They include pouched mammals, such as kangaroos and koalas, and egg-laying mammals, such as duck-billed platypuses. Eucalyptuses are the most famous Australian trees.

◁◁ Sydney, the largest city in Australia, has a famous opera house shaped like sails.

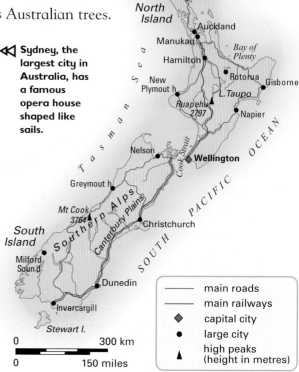

Legend:
- ── main roads
- ── main railways
- ◆ capital city
- ● large city
- ▲ high peaks (height in metres)

0 ——— 300 km
0 ——— 150 miles

The people

Most Australians live in towns and cities on the east coast. Sheep and cattle farming is important in New Zealand and Australia. The Australian outback also has coal and opal mines.

Pacific islanders depend on fishing, farming and tourism. Coconuts are an important crop.

▽ Uluru (Ayers Rock), in the outback, is a sacred mountain for Australian Aborigines.

▽ Coconut palms on the island of Lifou, New Caledonia. The coconuts are harvested for their oil.

Settling Oceania

Aborigines arrived in Australia at least 45,000 years ago. The Pacific islands were settled about 5000 years ago.

Around 1000 years ago Maori people from Polynesia discovered New Zealand. Europeans came to Oceania in the 1600s.

Arctic and Antarctica

The Arctic and Antarctica are the coldest places on the planet. The Arctic is the area around the North Pole. Most of it is a huge frozen ocean.

Antarctica is the continent around the South Pole. It is covered by a vast sheet of ice, built up over millions of years.

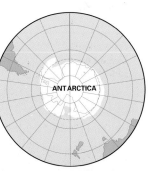

ANTARCTICA

KEY DATES

1909 American Robert Peary believes he reaches the North Pole

1911 Norwegian Roald Amundsen reaches the South Pole

1912 Captain Scott and his team die returning from the South Pole

1926 Amundsen flies over the North Pole in an airship

1968 American Ralph Plaisted is first to definitely reach the North Pole

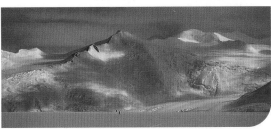

△ Antarctica has tall peaks, but they are mostly buried under the ice.

△ Polar bears live in the Arctic. They are fast runners and excellent swimmers.

Life in the Arctic

The land around the Arctic Ocean is flat and treeless. In summer the snow melts and plants grow. There is grazing for reindeer and musk oxen.

A few peoples live in the Arctic, including the Inuit, Sami and Chukchi. They traditionally live by fishing and keeping reindeer.

Antarctica

A few scientists live and work on Antarctica. Otherwise the continent is almost empty of life. In places the ice is over 3 kilometres thick.

The ocean around Antarctica contains millions of tiny creatures called krill. They feed fish, seals, penguins and whales.

country boundary
ice cap
sea covered by ice all year
sea covered by ice for part of the year

0 — 1000 km
0 — 500 miles

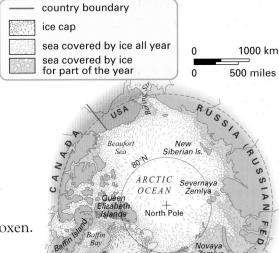

187

Acknowledgements

Edited by Clare Hibbert/Designed by Tinstar Design

The publishers would like to thank the following for permission to use their material. Every care has been taken to trace copyright holders. However, if there have been unintentional omissions or failure to trace copyright holders, we apologise, and will, if informed, endeavour to make corrections in any future edition.

Key
t = top; b = bottom; c = centre; r = right; l = left;
back = background; fore = foreground

ARTWORK

Allington, Sophie: 37b.
Arlott, Norman: 37cl.
Baker, Julian: 39tr; 83br.
Baum, Julian: 49tl; 67t; 67b; 71bl.
Beckett, Brian (Gecko Ltd): 28br.
Birkett, Georgie: 90l; 93cl.
Bull, Peter: 89br; 95br; 152cl.
Connolly, Peter: 135bl; 136b; 144br.
Cottam, Martin: 113tr.
Courtney, Michael: 12c; 14c.
D'Achille, Gino: 131tl; 131bcr.
Gaffney, Michael: 37tr.
Gecko Ltd: 6t; 77cr (James Sneddon); 91b; 97cr; 107cl.
Gulbis, Stephen: 78b; 84c; 98r.
Hadler, Terry: 92bl; 92r.
Hardy, David: 64tr; 69tr; 69b; 149cr.
Haslam, John: 51bl; 72tr; 87br.
Hawken, Nick: 62br; 88br.
Hinks, Gary: 48bl; 50tr; 50br; 52tr; 53c; 54b; 55br; 56tr; 59cr; 60br; 61tr.
Hiscock, Karen: 23tr.
Hook, Richard: 95tr; 145cl.

Jones Sewell Associates/ James Sneddon: 108bl.
Kennard, Frank: 10bl; 15cr.
Loates, Mick: 30; 31.
Madison, Kevin: 19br.
Mendez, Simon: 19c; 39bl.
Milne, Sean: 18b; 21cl; 23bl; 38c; 43bl; 43br; 57cl; 61b; 118br.
Ovendon, Denys: 35cl.
Oxford Designers and Illustrators: 71cr; 73r; 75bl; 80b; 87cl; 93r.
Oxford Illustrators/James Sneddon: 164tl.
Oxford University Press: 140bl.
Parsley, Helen (John Martin and Artists): 13c; 13br; 14br; 64br; 134tr.
Polley, Robbie (Virgil Pomfret): 79; 106tr; 106bl; 130–131; 133tr; 141tr; 141cl.
Richardson, Paul: 28tr; 43cr; 40tl; 44c; 45; 46t.
Roberts, Steve: 25; 27; 29tr; 32tr; 32cl; 33; 38cr; 38cl; 38br; 41cr; 47c.
Robinson, Andrew: 34.
Sanders, Martin: 173.
Sanders, Michael: 7br; 8l; 11cr; 36r.
Seymore, Steve: 6l.

Sneddon, James: 16tr; 19tr back; 21br back; 24r back; 76cl; 80c; 82cl; 86tr; 88r; 96br; 99cr; 100r; 101bl; 102; 103; 109cl; 119tr; 122bl; 123tr.
Visscher, Peter: 19tr fore; 20tr; 20br; 21br fore; 22tr; 24r fore; 26; 55bl; 125br; 127bl; 128br.
Ward, Catherine (Simon Girling Associates): 110b.
Weston, Steve: 7t; 8tr; 8br; 9tr; 10tr; 11bl; 15b; 17bl.
Wiley, Terry: 35r.
Woods, Michael: 32b.
Woods, Rosemary: 104cl.

PHOTOGRAPHS

Cover photos:
istockphoto.com.

Inside photos:
Aardman Animations Ltd 1993: 111tr.
Action Plus Photographic: 122tr (Glyn Kirk); 128tr (Glyn Kirk); 129tl (Glyn Kirk); 124tr (Al Messerschmidt); 124br (Chris Barry); 126bl (Mike Hewitt).
Ancient Art and Architecture: 114tl (R. Sheridan); 134br.
Heather Angel: 78cl.
Apple Computer Inc.: 112br.
Bibliothèque Royale Albert 1er, Brussels: 139br (BR13076.77, f24).
Bridgeman Art Library: 17cr (Lauros-Giraudon); 104br (Arthur Rackham Estate/Chris Beetles Ltd); 105tr (British Library); 105br (Fitzwilliam Museum, University of Cambridge); 114bl (Private Collection);

115tr (© Succession Picasso/DACS, 1998); 115bl (ADAGP Paris and DACS London, 1998); 135tr (Vatican Museum and Galleries, Vatican City, Italy); 135br (Museo e Gallerie Nazionali Di Capodimonte Naples); 137tl (Giraudon); 143tr (British Library); 146cr (Private Collection); 146br (British Library); 150cr; 151bl; 154tr (British Library); 164br (Palazzo Pitti, Florence).
British Airways: 92tr.
Bubbles Photo Library: 83cl (Loisjoy Thurston).
Christie's Images: 173tl.
Christo 1983: 114br (Wolfgang Volz).
The Coca-Cola Company: 112tr.
Corbis: 89tr (Ralph White).
Corel: 138b.
Haddon Davies: 81bl.
Dickens House Museum: 105bl.
Electricité de France/Michel Brigaud: 84tl.
E. T. Archive: 146bl; 152cr.
Mary Evans: 11tr; 109tl; 140br; 143cr; 172tr; 180br.
Mary Evans/Explorer: 142tr (Plisson).
The Exploratory, Bristol: 87tr.
Robert Francis: 127tl.
Geo Science Features/Dr B. Booth: 54tr; 54cr; 55cr.
Getty Images: 58bl (Mitch Kezar); 66br (Oldrich Karasek); 78cr; 99tr (Bob Thomas); 112cl (Michael Rosenfeld); 113r (Steven Weinberg); 117br (Nabeel Turner); 121c; 145cr; 149tl; 151tr; 153cr; 154cl; 154br

(David Young-Wolff); 158tr (Jerry Alexander); 163l (Natalie Fobes); 168br; 173bl. **Sally and Richard Greenhill:** 12br. **Greenpeace:** 96b (Sims). **The Guardian:** 100cl (Don McPhee). **Robert Harding:** 16bl (Adam Woolfitt); 16br (Liba Taylor); 23tl (T. Waltham); 29tl (N. A. Callow); 29cr (N. A. Callow); 53br (Lorraine Wilson); 59tr (Michael J. Howell); 74br (Financial Times); 75tr (Michael Short); 79l (M. Leslie Evans); 94t (J. H. C. Wilson); 116cl (Adam Woolfitt); 116br (Alain Evrard); 117tl (A.S.A.P.); 120br (Advertasia); 136cr (D. Beatty); 137br (Teresa Black); 139cl (Peter Scholey); 148bl (G. Renner); 155bl (Paolo Koch); 159t (Gavin Hellier); 161cl (David Martyn Hughes); 164tr (Philip Craven); 165tr; 165cl (Robert Frerck); 166tr (John Miller); 168l (Thomas Laird); 169cl (Nevada Wier); 169bl (Gavin Hellier); 171r (Gavin Hellier); 171bl (Schuster); 177bl (Simon Harris); 183tl (G. Renner); 185cr (Julian Pottage). **Michael Holford:** 108cl; 114tr; 132cl; 132tr; 133cl; 134bl; 135c; 140tr (Adam Woolfitt); 149tr. **Image Bank:** 24b (Margaret Mead); 61tl (Jeff Hunter); 62tr (Yiu Chun Ma); 77bl (Marc Romanelli); 79br (Walter Bibikow); 80r (Alan Choijnet); 113l (Alvis Upitis); 119b (Chris Hackett); 164cl

(Marc Romanelli); 170 (J. Du Bisberran); 174bl (Stuart Dee); 175cl (Andre Gallant); 176cl; 186tl (Peter Hendrie). **Images Colour Library:** 40bl. **Images of Africa:** 6br (Johann Van Tonder); 88bl (David Keith Jones); 118 (David Keith Jones); 184tl (Vanessa Burger). **Images of India:** 42tr; 120cl (Michael Ravinder). **Japan Information and Cultural Centre:** 106br. **Katz/Mansell Collection:** 106cr. **David King Collection:** 120tr; 153cl; 155tr; 155br. **Kobal:** 109cr (Paramount); 110tr (United Artists); 110cl (Selznick/MGM). **Museum of Fine Arts, Boston/William Sturgis Bigelow Collection:** 104tr. **MVP Munich:** 90bl. **NASA:** 48tr; 65t; 66tr; 66cl; 68tr; 68cl; 68br; 69cl; 70bl; 81r; 86br. **National Geographic Image Collection:** 56cl (George F. Mobley); 107bl (Volkmar Kurt Wentzel); 138cl (Stephen L. Alvarez); 145br (Kenneth Garrett). **National Maritime Museum:** 143bl. **Natural History Photographic Agency:** 20cl (Daniel Heuclin); 21tr (John Shaw); 22cl (John Shaw); 22br (Laurie Campbell); 24cl (B. Jones & M. Simlock); 27b (G. I. Bernard); 28l (Anthony Bannister); 29bl (John Shaw); 31br (Norbert Wu); 35bl (Daniel Heuclin); 36b (Stephen Dalton); 37tl (E. A.

Janes); 37bl (Manfred Danegger); 38tr (Stephen Dalton); 40cr (Stephen Krasemann); 41tr (John Shaw); 42bl (Anthony Bannister); 43tr (Christophe Ratier); 45t (Kevin Schafer); 56br (Anthony Bannister); 57tr (Rod Plank); 59bl (John Shaw); 63r (David Woodfall); 78tr (Stephen Krasemann); 97cl (Andy Rouse); 118tr (Douglas Dickens); 183cl (Nigel Dennis); 187tl (Jonathan Chester). **Peter Newark's Pictures:** 177br. **Oxford Scientific Films:** 58cr (Martyn Colbeck). **Oxford University Press:** 60cl; 71tl; 72bl; 72br; 73tl; 74tr; 76tr; 76br; 77br; 82tr; 82br; 84br; 85tr; 86tl; 90tr; 90br; 95bl; 96tr; 101cr; 121br; 122br; 123br; 124cl; 125tl; 126tr; 126 cr; 127cl; 127r; 128cl; 129bl; 129br; 158cl; 158b; 159r; 159bl; 161tr; 162r; 163tr; 165br; 166cl; 168cr; 169tr; 169cr; 171tl; 174tl; 175bl; 178cl; 179l; 179cr; 180tr; 183cr; 183b; 184tr; 184bl; 186cr; 186bl; 187bl. **Ann & Bury Peerless:** 116tr. **Planet Earth Pictures:** 44br (Geoff du Feu). **Popperfoto:** 123cl (Sam Mircovich); 152tr; 154bl (Juda Ngwenya, Reuters); 178br. **Redferns:** 107tr (Pankan Shar). **Rex Features:** 162cl. **The Royal Photographic Society, Bath:** 97tr. **Peter Sanders:** 117tr.

Science Photo Library: 10br (Ken Eward); 12tl; 17tl (Mark Clarke); 18tr (John Reader); 18cl (Sinclaire Stammers); 62cl (NOAA); 63bl; 64bl (David Parker); 67cl (NASA); 70tr; 72cl (Richard Folwell); 73bl (Dr George Gornacz); 74cl (Martin Dohrn); 75br; 77tr (James King-Holmes); 82bl (Peter Menzell); 85bl (Alex Bartel/SPL); 87bl (Will & Deni McIntyre); 91l (David Parker); 96cl; 98bl; 99bl (James King-Holmes); 99br (Nelson Morris); 148cr (Dr Jeremy Burgess); 149bl (Los Alamos National Laboratory); 149br (Philippe Plailly/Eurelios). **Space Charts Photo Library:** 65b. **Peter Spilsbury:** 117bl. **Still Pictures:** 57br (Daniel Dancer). **South American Pictures:** 109tr; 179br; 180tl; 180bl. **Suzuki:** 94cl. **Tate Gallery:** 115br (ADAGP Paris and DACS London, 1998). **Topham:** 52br (Y. Shimbun). **Topham Picture Source:** 184br (G. Marinovich). **Trek Bikes:** 94b. **The Walt Disney Company Limited:** 176t. **Woodfall Wild Images:** 43cl (Steve Austin); 50cl. **WWF:** 47b. **York Archaeological Trust:** 144cr.

Index

Page numbers in **bold** mean that this is where you will find the most information on that subject. If both a heading and a page number are in bold, there is an article with that title. A page number in *italic* means that there is a picture of that subject. There may also be other information about the subject on the same page.